RELIGIONS AROUND THE WORLD

BY

LEONARD AND CAROLYN WOLCOTT

DRAWINGS BY
GORDON LAITE

GEOFFREY CHAPMAN
LONDON DUBLIN MELBOURNE 1970

Geoffrey Chapman Ltd
18 High Street, Wimbledon, London SW 19

Geoffrey Chapman (Ireland) Ltd
5–7 Main Street, Blackrock, Co. Dublin

Acknowledgment

We wish to express our thanks to the following persons who read portions of the manuscript and made helpful suggestions: the Reverend Xenophon Diamond, archdiocesan office, Greek Orthodox Church; Dr. Charles E. Fuller, Scarritt College; Dr. Winston King, Vanderbilt University; the Reverend Herbert Rogers, S.J., Fordham University; Dr. Lou Silberman, Vanderbilt University; the Reverend John Sfikas, Greek Orthodox Church; Dr. Simon Ting, Philippine Christian College; Dr. Vipin B. Trivedi, The M. S. University of Baroda; Dr. J. Christy Wilson, Emeritus, Princeton University.

The authors and publishers are indebted to the following for photographs which are used with permission: **American Bible Society**—page 147 lower right. **Arabian American Oil Company**—page 163 top. **Boeing Overseas Airways Corporation**—page 147 lower left. **Chinese Information Service**—page 83 bottom. **Toge Fujihira**—pages 25; 43 upper left; 62; 79; 98; 163 middle left; and 187 top. **Information Service of India**—page 43 upper right. **Japanese National Tourist Organization**—pages 15 and 105. **Leon V. Kofod**—page 28 bottom. **Methodist Prints** (Department of Visual Education, 475 Riverside Drive, New York)—pages 12 upper right; and 163 bottom. **Nashville Banner**—page 127. **Newark Museum**—page 9. **Religious News Services**—pages 116 lower left; and 147 top. **Three Lions**—pages 12 upper left; 83 upper; 116 upper left by Al Barry; upper right by George Pickow; lower right by John Dominis; and 163 middle right. **Trans World Airlines**—pages 12 lower right; and 28 top. **United Nations**—page 43 lower left. **Edward Wallowich**—page 187 bottom. **Wide World Photos, Inc.**—page 157.

This edition first published in the United Kingdom, 1970
Copyright © 1967 by Abingdon Press
ISBN 0 225 65837 2
Printed in Great Britain by A. Wheaton & Company, Exeter

Reservation — of p 146
p 155

Contents

Time

The most universally recognized calendar in use today designates time as either B.C., meaning "before Christ," or A.D., anno Domini, meaning "in the year of our Lord," and referring to the approximate date of the birth of Jesus. In this book B.C. and A.D. will be used to identify all dates. In some parts of the world, however, other calendars, based on events in other religions, are in use in those areas where the majority of the people belong to one of those religions.

I
Beginning
Religion

Our Believing World

Everyone believes in something.

Some believe in a world of unseen spirits that can help them or harm them. Some believe in many gods who can be flattered into giving them what they want. Some believe in their own ability to make a happier world. Some believe in science, some in history, and others in philosophical speculation. Some believe in one just God who demands uprightness among his people. They may believe in a God who loves all his people and expects them to live in good-will for each other. Wherever people are in the world, whether they live in tribes or in great modern cities, they believe in something. Belief is part of being a human being. Our world is a believing world.

The Search for Answers

What makes a leaf stir when there is hardly a breeze? What makes the thunder roar and the rain fall? Where does the sun go when it sets? What is the mystery of the mountains? What does life mean?

Do you know?

Once people did not know. Once *science* had

few answers. Once *religion* had few answers. Men looked for answers. If they could not find answers they thought up stories to explain the mysteries of the universe.

Long ago man made a great scientific discovery. He discovered fire. Long ago man also made a great religious discovery. He discovered there exists in the world power greater than man's power and greater than the power of nature. *Spirit* is a name for this power.

With his knowledge of fire man cooked food, made utensils, and protected himself from wild animals. With his discovery of spirit man found ways to worship, made rules for living, and learned to become more than an animal.

Early man kept his eyes and ears open to see and hear the world around him. He knew many things about nature that kept him alive in circumstances under which modern man might die.

Early man looked for answers to his questions about the world. His questions were mostly about his daily needs, but he also had questions about what life means. He wanted to keep trouble out of his life. But he also wanted to know why there was trouble in the world. His struggle with nature was early science. His attempt to understand what was behind nature was early religion. Science helped him find ways to meet his needs. Religion helped him explain the world of nature and people about him. Early man often used *myths* to explain his experiences. Myths are explanations of experiences and events people do not completely understand. Some myths told of animals or heroes or ancestors. Some explained the creation of the world and the coming and going of the seasons. A few explained why man must work, suffer, die. Most myths were poetic and imaginative.

Many people of all times have looked for answers about the meaning of their experiences and have been aware of a power greater than the power of nature.

A World of Power

Early man most often considered anything unusual as evidence of supernatural power: unusual shapes, bright colours, high mountains, deep craters, strong animals, waterfalls, earthquakes, volcanoes. Supernatural power, they believed, could take control of anything, large or small. It could control anybody and make him do unusual things. Sometimes such power stayed permanently in a person or object. Sometimes it came and went. It could never be seen, but it was always somewhere. It could be helpful, but it could also be dangerous.

The Crowded Unseen World

For many people in the past, the unseen world was crowded. Ghosts of ancestors wandered about. Spirits with wills of their own lurked in dark places. There were spirits in animals, in trees and vegetables, in stones and sticks, in the dust of the air. Some people made *symbols* or *idols* to represent the spirits or gods. Some people in parts of the world today, such as Indians in the Andes Mountains of South America, reverence rocks and lakes and caves. They say spirits live in them as well as in rivers and in the mountains. Bedouins in Arabia have said that there are spirits who live in strangely shaped rocks and in water springs. The villagers of India say the spirits come out at midnight to sit on the leaves of the sacred pipal tree.

Many people have believed that their ancestors joined the unseen spirit world. Some Africans believed that their ancestors were always near, in the shadows. Ancestors, they thought, never went very far from the place where they had lived. Great-grandfather, after he died, stayed by his family watching them. Some African tribes have thought ancestors wandered in a jungle in the land of shades, then came back to the homes of their descendants. People of old China and Japan wanted to live where their ancestors had lived. If a family moved, its members returned from time to time to honour their ancestors.

7

Many early people believed in a god who was a distant, mysterious being. Different tribes had different names for this god. Ancient people in the land of the Tigris and Euphrates east of the Mediterranean Sea, called their god a father. So did early Romans and early Australians. Some American tribes called him the Great Father. Some African tribes thought of him as an old, old man. The Chinese and many of the people of ancient India and ancient Greece called him the Sky. Some South American tribes gave him no name at all. He was too great to be called by any name. It was this high god, some thought, who may have started the creation of other gods, and the creation of the world and people.

Many people have believed that the unseen world was always affecting their lives. In their dreams and in their imagination the unseen world seemed very real. For them, everything they could see, smell, hear, or touch had religious meaning. Many tribal people believed that, as each person was part of his own tribe, so each tribe had its own spirits that could help or harm.

Dealing with the Unseen World

Early science tried to discover what caused trouble, or why people became sick, or where disease came from. People knew only that sometimes trouble pounced on them. Many associated their troubles with *demons.* So they put spots on their foreheads, signs on their doorposts, symbols on their doors, curves on their roofs, or pots in their fields to protect themselves, their houses, or their gardens from troublesome unseen spirits. In Thailand, people still set up spirit houses to keep the spirits contented. They believe the spirits own the land.

Many believed that sickness and trouble came when the spirits were offended. Spirits and gods of disease could be angered by some accidental act, they thought. Then the gods or spirits sent sickness to punish them. *Witches,* they believed, were people who could command evil spirits to make them ill or even to kill them.

▶ Among the Yoruba people of Nigeria the god of thunder, Shango, is shown with a double axe on his head. Similar axe-shaped stones found on the ground are explained as thunderbolts dropped from the sky.

Ancestors, many thought, had power that people on earth do not have. Some tribes built *shrines* for their dead. Some buried their dead in such a way that they could not get up and go wandering about making trouble. In East Asia, families still write the names of their ancestors on tablets and place them on a special shelf in the house. They greet the ancestors each morning and offer them flowers or a bit of food.

But the unseen world was not always harmful. It could be helpful. Not only were there bad spirits, there were good spirits. Not only did ancestor spirits punish those who neglected them. They helped those who honoured them. Not only could supernatural power destroy. It could benefit those who knew how to use it. But who knew how to use it? Only the skilled specialist knew. A name for this specialist is *shaman*. Sometimes he is called a *medicine man*.

The shaman or medicine man was the early doctor. He used whatever science he knew, and magic was part of his science. *Magic* was an important medicine in dealing with the spirit world. Magic, people believed, could keep sickness away when anyone wore a charm around his neck, wrist, waist, or ankle. Magic could keep a house from harm when a charm was hung from the rafters or placed on the doorpost. Magic mixtures, when drunk, could make people fall in love. They could bring babies. Proper magic ceremonies could make rain fall. Sometimes the spirit specialist used magic numbers, magic sounds and syllables to command the spirit world. Sometimes he used diagrams and images. There were magic medicines such as rare bird feathers, horns of deer, teeth of bears or leopards, skulls of cats, dried bats, snakes, or rats. Some people in the world still use these medicines.

Medicine men, wise men, or priests said they could look into the future and foretell what was going to happen. Some forecast the future by the number and direction of flying birds. Some forecast events by studying the internal organs of animals they had sacrificed. Others went into a trance and spoke *oracles*—words from the spirit world.

Sometimes a powerful unseen spirit seemed to take possession of the spirit specialist and control everything he did. In many tribes a medicine man, a priest, or the chief chanted prayers to gods. The chanted prayers, they thought, were useful in getting the gods to protect the tribe.

Sometimes the medicine man or priest threatened a god in order to get his help. Sometimes they punished the god because he had not done what they had requested. More often, however, they flattered the god or bribed him with a sacrifice to please him. They reasoned that when the god was pleased he had to do what they wanted him to do.

Sacrifice has been important, and for many people, it still is. In sacrifice they give to the gods something they themselves like. They reason, "If we give up what we like the gods will give us what we want." In sacrifice the people give the gods fresh flowers, bright colours, or good food. Sometimes they leave food on a mountain or in a desert place so the gods and spirits may eat the essence of the food in the dark. Sometimes they burn the food so the smoke will carry it to the gods. Sometimes they kill an animal and give the animal and its lifeblood to the gods. The priests, and occasionally the people, eat the food that is offered. This is sharing with the god that which the god has made holy. Sometimes people in the past even sacrificed children. What god, they have thought, could resist such a sacrifice!

Some early people worshipped their gods and tried to please the spirits so that the gods and spirits would give good hunting to the hunters, good crops to the farmers, many lambs to their sheep, and calves to their cows. They would try to get the gods to help them win their battles and their wars.

Worship often took the form of feasts and dances and merrymaking by all the people. Feasts were a sharing with the gods. Dances influenced the gods, they thought. Merrymaking and noisemaking scared away the demons.

11

▲   A spirit-possessed medium coming out of a trance.

▲   Wood-carved god of the winds at the gate of a shrine in Japan. His fierce appearance is intended to scare away evil spirits.

▶   A masked devil dancer of Nepal.

Living Together

There is a science that has to do with the way people live together. People follow customs and make rules to regulate their life together. Without rules and customs to guide them, no one can live at peace. The rules of early people were the beginning of systems of law. So important were the rules, that most people considered that the world of spirit was interested in seeing that the rules were obeyed.

Important rules of the *tribe* or *clan* have had to do with whom a person might marry or might not marry, or with what anyone might touch or might not touch. If anyone ate or touched something forbidden, he might die of fright believing that to eat something forbidden could be as disastrous as drinking poison.

Often, when someone broke a rule, he had to perform a special ceremony to the gods of his people. Until he did, no one among his people would have anything to do with him. When anyone, for example, did something which his tribe considered unclean, he had to take a ceremonial bath. Until he did, the tribe considered him unclean.

Many tribal people have had stories about great bears or great heroes, or even small animals or vegetables which represented their tribe or clan. Sometimes they told stories about the heroes who started their tribe or clan. Some claimed that their clan was descended from a hero who had special power.

Many believed their clan was related to an animal—a beaver, bear, wolf, or cricket—or a plant. The animal or plant distinguished their family or clan from other families and clans in the tribe. This is called *totemism*. A totem group sometimes had its own special ceremonies connected with its respect for the animal or vegetable that represented the group. At special festivals Indians in America today may dress as animal, bird, or human heroes; and in plays and dances tell the legends of their tribe. Poles with carvings of the clan's animals have been found in Canada and in Alaska.

13

The World We Live In

Science has come a long way from the magic of the medicine man. Yet many early scientific ideas are still held by people today. Religion has come a long way from the worship of spirits in rocks and trees, stones and streams. Yet many ideas of early religion are still found in the world today. These early scientific and religious ideas are found on all the continents and in many of the islands of the sea. Some people wear good luck charms. Others try to get God to make them well or rich or happy. In Korea the medicine man is often a woman called a *mudong*. People pay her, especially when they are sick, to get in touch with the spirit world to heal them.

In Japan, many people follow *Shinto* which means "the way of the gods." The gods are the *Kami*. Anything which appears to have supernatural power or some strange or unusual form, or great beauty—a volcano, a river, a flowering tree—the Japanese may call Kami. Kami, they believe, are in the mountains, and in the forests, in waterfalls, in rugged cliffs beside the sea. Kami can be anywhere in nature, in animals, and in man. Japanese Shinto has many legends to explain the creation of the Kami and of the Japanese Islands. The legends say that the Japanese emperor is descended from the sun goddess, *Amaterasu*.

A Shinto shrine stands in almost every Japanese village and city. The men in charge of the temples honour the Kami of Japan and perform marriage ceremonies. Many Japanese make pilgrimages to Shinto shrines that are especially famous. They come to worship or simply to admire the beauty of the shrines and their gardens.

Since the first answer to men's questions about the world, science has discovered what makes a leaf stir and the rain fall and the thunder roar, where the sun goes when it sets, how the mountains were formed, what causes disease, and many other things. Yet some people still cling to early scientific ideas.

Since its first explanations about life, religion has made discoveries about who we are, what life is all about, and how to live together. Religion has helped people understand themselves and God's meaning in their lives. Yet some people still cling to early religious ideas. Some early ideas are held by some people in all the world's great religions.

World Religions

There are still tribal religions in the world. A *tribal religion* is one which is followed by one group in one place.

But there are also great *world religions*. These are religions that are practiced by people of many different nations, with many different customs, and many different languages.

There are two types of world religions. One type emphasizes *man's experience* in his search for truth. Hinduism and Buddhism (which came out of Hinduism) are this kind of religion. The other type emphasizes *God's revelation of himself* to man and man's response to God. Judaism, and Christianity and Islam (both of which are partly built on Judaism) are this second type of religion.

How did the great religions come to be? What explanations do they give about life? What do their followers believe? That is what the following chapters are about.

► Shinto shrine on the Island of Miyajima, near Hiroshima City.

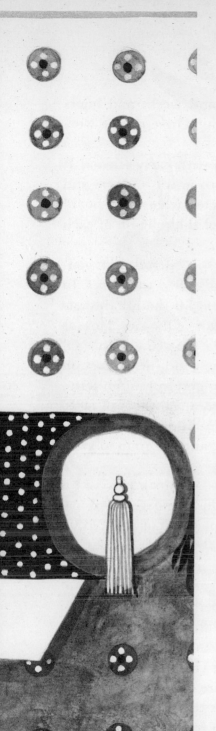

II
Religions
of Long Ago

Forty Centuries Ago

Four thousand years ago in Europe, Africa, and Asia there were forests, meadows, and mountains but no cities—except, that is, along five rivers.

Beside these rivers and nearby, men built villages, towns, and cities with shops, schools, and palaces.

There was the Nile River that flows north from Central Africa through lakes and plains and desert to the Mediterranean Sea.

There were the Tigris and Euphrates rivers which flow from the mountains of western Asia south east to the Persian Gulf.

From the Tigris and Euphrates plains men took ideas of civilization to people along the Indus River in the western part of the great subcontinent of Asia. This river rises in Tibet and flows through West Pakistan to the Arabian Sea.

And far away to the east, the *Hwang Ho*—the Yellow River—winds its way through northern China from west to east.

Along these river valleys men first discovered how to read and write. They learned about mathematics and studied the stars. Here they

17

made calendars to divide the time into years and weeks and hours according to the movement of the sun and moon. These people worshipped many gods in many temples.

Their religion, like early religion, was mixed with early science. It was also mixed with politics, for to be a good citizen was to serve and obey the city or village god. Their religion directed what they should do and what they should not do. At the head of the religion of each city or town were the king and the priests.

Each city and town and village had its own special gods and goddesses. In some places the chief god was simply called the Chief. In some cities he was called the Father from whom all the inhabitants were thought to have descended. He was protector of the city. He was leader in its wars. He represented power greater than any man's. Of all the people, the king was thought to be closest to him. In fact, in some places, the king was even thought to be a god in human form.

The people looked upon the goddesses as great mothers of gods. Goddesses, they were sure, made it possible for children to be born, for cows to have calves, for sheep to have lambs, and for grain to grow in the fields.

A good farmer ploughed and sowed his fields and took care of his flock. But he did more. He worshipped the gods and goddesses of fields and flocks that they might make the grass plentiful and the grain grow.

A good business man bought and sold goods and took care of his money. But he did more. He worshipped the gods and goddesses of trade and luck that they might bring him prosperity.

A good soldier marched, fought, shot arrows, and threw spears. But he did more. He worshipped the god of war and the goddess of his city that they might protect him in battle and bring victory in war.

A good mother nursed her babies and took care of her husband. But she did more. She prayed to the household gods that they might keep the members of the family safe and guard them from harm.

Farmers, businessmen, soldiers, and housewives all believed that without the help of the gods nothing would go well. Faith in the gods made them better farmers, better businessmen, better soldiers, better housewives. To forget to worship the gods was to bring disaster.

River City Religion

In the land of the Tigris and Euphrates rivers the people built skyscraper-temples for the worship of their gods. These were man-made mountains of sun-dried brick. Their name, *ziggurat*, meant "top of a mountain." The ziggurats were great pyramids of steps with ramps running to a shrine on the top. Up these ramps marched the priests to offer gifts to the god of their city.

There were many gods to watch over the people—gods of heaven, earth and water, gods of sun and moon. Priests studied the constellations in the skies to understand how the stars influenced people. Most popular was a mother-goddess. Also popular was the father-god. The people honoured the bull because he represented energy and the on-going of life. The worship of the bull was also found along the Nile River in the west, and the Indus River in the east.

In the land of the Nile River, priests made offerings to the river, for without the river crops would not grow and no one could live. The river flooded the fields each year with new, rich soil brought from distant parts of Africa. The river was a highway for travel. The people who lived along the Nile were grateful to the river-god who they believed made life possible. If they forgot to worship the river, they reasoned, the river might forget to help them.

The Egyptians wondered what happened after death. They had a *Book of the Dead* which gave spells and magic recitations to make life after death happy. But life after death, they were afraid, would not be happy for everyone. The hearts of the dead were weighed by the gods. If a man's heart was heavy with the evil he had done he was punished. If his heart was light he was ready to go to the land of happiness with

his god. The kings, priests, and rich people built great tombs in which
to be buried. They furnished these with everything they thought might
be needed in the land of the dead. They left slits in the tombs so the
souls could go in and out. Near the tombs the kings built temples where priests said prayers for them. On tomb and temple walls
they painted reminders of their goodness and greatness.

Each town in Egypt had its own animal-headed god such as a cat,
a jackal, a hawk, a vulture, a crocodile, an ibis, a ram, a bull, or a
lioness. When Egypt became a great empire one of her kings, *Ikhnaton,*
tried to get all the people to worship one supreme God, *Aton,* represented by the sun.

In the land of the Indus River in India, a civilization like that of
the Tigris and Euphrates grew up. The people worshipped the bull and
other gods, one of whom, they thought, had power to give them life
and prosperity. This god could also destroy them, so they worshipped
him to keep him contented.

In the land of the Hwang Ho an ancient city, Loyang, became the
centre of a Chinese kingdom. The people honoured the sky, studied the
stars, and thought that in all nature there lived helpful and harmful
spirits. The ancient Chinese made magic signs, puzzles, and ceremonies
to control the spirits.

Along five river systems of the world great civilizations grew. And
in these civilizations religion was an important part of daily life.

Forest Religion

Like the people living in the river towns, those who lived in forests
and fields and on mountains believed in many gods. There was
so much to wonder at—around them, above them, below them. Whatever puzzled them they associated with a god. There was the sky
above, wider than the world. There were the sun and moon moving
through the sky. No one could explain the sky or the sun or the moon.
"But," said the people, "life depends on them." So they called sky,

sun, and moon, gods. They were especially grateful for the sun with its life-giving warmth. Many worshipped the sun as it rose each morning. Others said of the sky, "Sky is the greatest god because it is over everything."

The winds blew and the rain fell. No one could explain the power of the wind so they called the wind a god. No one could explain the thunder that sometimes came with the rain, or the rainbow that arched the sky. They believed the rain must be a thundering god of war, the rainbow his bow.

Under them was the earth. They saw that when anything died it decayed into the earth. "Earth is a god, too, and the god of death belongs to earth," they decided. On earth was the wonder of fire. Fire could burn and destroy. But it could also cook their food and turn their offerings into smoke that rose to the gods in the skies. They could not explain the marvel of fire, and they called it a god.

But many said, "Sky which is over everything is the true god!"

These gods are *nature gods*. The people who believed in them thought that they were not only powerful, but personal. To them, Sun and Moon, Earth and Fire, and other natural wonders were really persons —strange and powerful persons. Storytellers told tales about the feasts of these gods, about their marriages and their wars. They told about their great hunts and battles, music-making, and crafts. These gods, then, were important to people as they themselves feasted, married, waged war, as they hunted, made music, and followed their crafts.

Vigorous, warlike Aryan tribes living near the Caspian Sea believed in these nature gods. From their homeland these tribes moved west, north, and south in Europe. Some went as far as the sea coasts of western Europe and crossed to the British Isles. Others moved south west to the hills of Asia Minor and built the Hittite nation into a great empire. Some pushed even farther south and settled in Egypt for a time. Others moved east to the plains north of Persia, and others went south into the country now called by their name, Iran (from Aryan). Still

21

others moved east and south and climbed through the high mountain passes to the plains of India.[1]

Wherever these tribal people went—west, south, east, or north—they carried with them their names for the gods of the sky, the air, the earth.

So the gods of the people who lived in Europe long ago and the gods of the people who lived in Asia were much the same. The gods of the Europeans and of the Greeks and Romans, the gods of the Persians and of the people who moved down into India resembled each other. There came a time, however, when the people of Europe and of south-west Asia and Persia gave up their belief in these many gods and began to believe in one God. In India, however, some of these ancient gods are still honoured.

God of Light

One day a preacher stood before the king of Persia. He told about one God—the God of skies, the God of wisdom and right. The preacher said, "Do not call everything you wonder at 'god.' There is only one God. He made you. He created everything that is good."

The king was interested. The people listened but pointed out there was much that was not good in the world.

The preacher agreed but declared that in time God would destroy all the bad in the world. "God has sent *Amesha Spentas*—spirits of good sense, of power and splendour, of piety and immortality—into the world," he explained. "The Amesha Spentas come from God, the *Wise Lord*. They are at war with the bad spirits who come from the *King of Lies*. In the end the Amesha Spentas, the good spirits, will be victorious and put an end to all that is bad in the world.

"You know what I am talking about," continued the preacher, "because in each of you there is a battle going on between a good conscience and bad desires." The preacher urged the people to cooperate

---

[1] Some writers of India believe that the Aryans originally came from India.

with the Amesha Spentas, the good spirits. He told the people that when good thoughts came to them then they would recognize the one God.

The preacher's name was *Zarathustra* (sometimes called *Zoroaster,* the Greek form of his name) and he lived in Persia probably during the seventh or sixth century B.C.[1] He called God by the name *Ahura Mazda* —Wise Lord. The King of Lies he called *Angra Mainyu.* Angra Mainyu stands for darkness, and Ahura Mazda stands for light.

"Light," said Zarathustra, "destroys darkness. Bad men do evil under cover of darkness. The old gods, the *daevas,* are really devils. These devils can work on people whose minds are without light. God, Ahura Mazda, brings light to their minds. God is like a fire," Zarathustra said. "God is bright. He makes dark places light. His burning light can burn up the rubbish in your minds. God will judge you one day, and his light will show up all the darkness in you."

Zarathustra gave advice for cooperating with the good spirits. He warned against lying, cheating, and drunkenness. He argued against a nomadic, wandering way of life. "Settle down in one place and work hard," he told the people. "Do what is right! Think good thoughts, speak good words, do good deeds. One day," he promised, "God will destroy all evil and set up a great kingdom for those who love him."

The people in Persia became believers in the religion of Zarathustra. His religion came to be called *Zoroastrianism.* For over a thousand years the Zoroastrians followed his teachings.

Then came an invading army of Arabs who brought with them a new faith, Islam, which gradually replaced the old religion of the Persians. A few Zoroastrians, however, escaped and went to China and to India. Descendants of these refugees still live in or near the city of Bombay in India. The Indians call them *Parsi,* or "Persians." On a hill above the city of Bombay stands a great *tower of silence.* When Zoroastrians die their bodies are laid out on a stone floor in this tower, exposed to the air—and to the ever watchful vultures. The soul goes

---

[1] No one is sure. Some people believe he lived three hundred years earlier, 1000 B.C.

to be with God, they say, and the body returns to the elements from which it has come.

The "Noble People"

The tribes who crossed the mountains into India were much like their relatives who went to Persia. They were tall, light-skinned, and like their Persian cousins, called themselves *Aryans*—"the Noble People." They were fighters and hunters. To reach the rich plains of northern India they had to cross high mountains. When they saw mountain peaks whose summits were almost always hidden by clouds, they fancied that the gods must live on the mountain-tops. When they followed streams that flowed from the mountains to the plains, they decided that the rivers came from the gods in the mountains.

For several months each year thunder rolled in the mountains and rain fell. The migrating tribes called the rain-god *Indra.* They thought he must be king of the gods. They asked his help when they went down the steep mountain slopes to fight and conquer the people of the plains. These Aryans coming over the mountains brought horses with them. Horses were their wealth. They depended upon them to defeat the foot-soldiers of the plains-people. When they wanted to win Indra's help in battle, they sacrificed their best horses to him. They poured butter on the burning sacrifice to make smoke that would rise to the god. They asked *Agni,* god of fire, to take their requests to the gods. They called upon Sun and Sky. And they called upon their *priests.*

The priests knew the proper way to make a sacrifice. They could repeat the magic syllables which would, they believed, make the gods listen. They could compose hymns that flattered the gods. They could win power from the gods for health, prosperity, and victory in war. The more they praised the gods, they thought, the better they could please the gods. The better the gods were pleased, the greater the help.

The priests taught the hymns to their sons. The sons taught them to their sons. Each family of priests had its own type of hymns. After

24

▲   Hindu worshipper at a shrine (India).

many years the hymns were written down. Each hymn praises one of the gods as though he were the only god. Many of these hymns are nearly three thousand years old. The oldest and first known collection of hymns is called the *Rig Veda*.

Demons, Gods, and Goddesses

People were living in the plains of India long before the Aryans came over the mountains. These people, called *Dravidians* (and still living in South India), were generally short, dark, and curly-haired. Even before the Dravidians, aboriginal tribes had lived in India's jungles.

The jungle tribes and the Dravidians suspected that in the world there were unseen demons which could harm them. When sickness came, they supposed that angry demon-goddesses were punishing them. Different goddesses brought different diseases. When sickness came to a village, the villagers sacrificed a goat to the goddess or placed rice before her shrine. They wanted to make her go away and take the disease with her. As the winter began, and at ploughing-time, they made offerings to a goddess hoping that she would not destroy their crops.

Most people around the world at some time in their history have feared such evil spirits. In India many still do.

Among the Dravidians were many wise men. Some were the doctors of medicine who knew the plants that could cure disease. Some were doctors of spirits who said they knew how to control and drive away demons. These doctors said that although demons were to be reckoned with, the most important thing in the whole world was *energy*. Without energy no one could undertake any task. Without energy plants would not grow, cows would not calve, and children would not be born.

Because energy was important to living, boys prayed to the monkey-god, called *Hanuman,* who was said to be stronger than anything or anybody in the world. They asked the monkey-god to make them strong, strong enough to win in wrestling matches with their friends.

Girls asked the goddesses, who represented God's energy, to give them strong husbands and many children. When farmers ploughed their fields they called on the name of *Shiva*, the source of energy. They called on Shiva's sturdy bull, *Nandi*, to give them many cows with rich milk. Shiva, it was said, was so powerful that when he danced the earth shook. Shiva could destroy all living things, but, if farmers honoured him and remembered him when they ploughed and sowed and harvested, he would not destroy but would give them good crops.

Many people in India still pray to the goddesses of sickness, to the monkey-god, and to Shiva.

Men Who Had Power

The *Brahmins* were the priests of the conquering Aryans. They were more powerful than chiefs and kings. All the people held them in awe because they thought the Brahmins could get what they wanted from the gods. The Brahmins were the men who conducted the sacrifice of horses, as they muttered magic syllables and chanted songs in praise of the gods. They were the men who wrote the hymns, the Vedas. They were the men who wrote the books and taught the people. They wrote the rules for religious ceremonies. They wrote the regulations that controlled a person's conduct from the time he was born until he died. They wrote books on politics, on society, and on science. They wrote books of stories. They wrote the longest book that was ever written, the *Mahabharata*, sometimes called *The Great Book of India*. It is like an encyclopedia of knowledge with fables and stories about early India.

New classes arose among the people according to the work they performed. Out of these classes came the later *castes* of Hinduism. At the top were the Brahmins who said they were next to the gods. Second came the kings and princes, the *Kshatriyas*, whose job it was to protect and govern the people. Next came the great mass of peasants and artisans, farmers, traders, and craftsmen, the *Vaishyas*. The people of these three groups were Aryans, the "Noble People." When a boy was

27

▲ Stone carving of Nandi, sacred bull of Shiva.

▲ Mounted heads of ancient Ba'al idols (the bull was a god of fertility).

born he was initiated into his group or caste. This initiation was called a second birth. So the people in the first three castes were called "twice-born." The twice-born looked down on the fourth caste, the *Shudras*. The fourth caste people were the Dravidians, the people of the plains whom the Aryans had conquered. They had to live in the Aryan towns and do the work for the upper castes. A legend says that the Brahmins came from the brain, the Kshatriyas from the arms, the Vaishyas from the stomach, and the Shudras from the feet of the supreme soul of the universe.

Men Who Were Hermits

There were wise men in India who believed that the only way to get hold of the powers of the universe was to live simply and endure hardship. The Brahmins often went off to the forests to live in communities with other Brahmins, or to live alone. Books, called *Thoughts for Forest Men—Aranyakas—*helped them meditate.

These hermits wore few clothes and ate little. They were exposed to rain, wind, heat, and cold. Ordinary people respected them and called them holy men. Some of the holy men lived such good lives that it was said the gods became concerned. "If we let these men go on living such unselfish lives," the gods declared, "we will have to give them everything they ask." So the gods sometimes tempted the holy men to forget their meditations, to eat fine food, or enjoy the company of pretty girls. To the holy men who ignored their temptations the gods said, "All right, you have stood firm. Ask of us whatever you wish."

Some holy men asked for peace and quiet. Some asked to be freed from existence in this world. Some asked for long life. Some even asked for the power of the gods. There is a well-known story in India about two brothers, *Kumbhakarana*—"One with ears like a pitcher," and *Ravana*—"Howler," who, as holy men, asked to be made so powerful and so strong that nothing, not even the gods, could kill them. Their wish was granted. Ravana became an unconquerable demon

29

king. Kumbhakarana developed an enormous appetite. He could, in one sitting, devour thousands of buffaloes and drink hundreds of barrels of wine. To satisfy his hunger, he ate thousands of men and horses until it looked as though nothing would be left. To save the world, it became necessary for the gods to put him to sleep for long periods.

Most holy men, however, were good men. The creatures of the forest trusted them. People came to them for advice. Kings left their palaces to ask their counsel. These holy men were interested only in understanding the unseen power behind all the universe and above all gods. They lived strict, simple lives and had no possessions to worry about.

Men Who Were Heroes

Most of the people of old India did not understand the religion of the Brahmins. They preferred stories of heroes. Their favourite heroes were a prince called *Rama* and a cowherd called *Krishna*.

Rama was the handsome hero prince whose kingdom of Kosala lay between the Himalayan Mountains and the Ganges River. He had won the hand of the beautiful princess *Sita* in a contest with other princes and kings. Rama and Sita lived happily together until Ravana, the ten-headed demon king of Ceylon, kidnapped the lovely princess. Rama, with the help of armies of forest tribes—called monkeys and bears in the story—bravely crossed the sea to the demon's island kingdom, fought and conquered the demon army, killed Ravana, and rescued Sita. When Rama returned home in triumph with Sita, the happy people of his capital city proclaimed them king and queen.

The story of Rama, found in a book called the *Ramayana,* is still the favourite tale of all India. Even outside India, in Thailand and the islands of Indonesia, Rama's story is acted out in plays and in dances. For centuries, every king of Thailand has been named Rama.

Krishna, the cowherd hero, grew from a dark-skinned chubby baby into a mischief-making boy who could do amazing feats. A story says that once, when Krishna's ball fell into the river, he jumped in to recover it and became entangled with a cobra snake. He beat the snake and came out dancing on its hood. When he grew to be a young man, Krishna spent long hours playing the flute while he took care of his cows. Krishna had the help of many pretty cowgirls. He was a favourite with everyone, for he was stronger, handsomer, and more clever than any other young man.

Gradually these two popular heroes came to be considered gods. Every Hindu boy and girl in India today knows the stories of Rama and Krishna.

Long Ago and Now

The religion of the ancient Dravidians, of the Brahmin priests, of hermit thinkers, and of the tellers of hero-stories, together made up the religion of old India.

These religions of long ago, however, are still found in India. On the street corners of cities like Bombay and Calcutta, in the high mountains of the north, and in the villages of the great plains, stand temples with idols of gods who have been worshipped longer than man can remember. Young students and old people, boys and girls, men and women, still worship them. Each joins his hands, palm to palm, and says his prayer before the image of one of India's many gods—gods in the forms of men, of women, of animals. A man will pray facing the rising sun while bathing in a river early in the morning. His ancestors have done this since ancient times. He makes an offering of flowers, or sweets, or money, or sometimes, fruit to his god. When he has prayed and made his offering he (or the priest) puts a mark of sandalwood paste on his forehead as a symbol in honour of his god. All who look at him know that he has worshipped.

The gods and goddesses, the temples and priests, the holy men and devout worshippers of old India are today part of the world religion of Hinduism. So it is that in Hinduism religious ideas and practices of an ancient people are still to be found.

31

III
Hindu
Religion

The Holy River

On hot plains, at the feet of snow-capped mountains, in jungles and hills, by the wide rivers of the Indian Peninsula in South Asia, the Hindu religion grew. It began before history was written.

The Ganges River is the greatest river in India. It is one of the large rivers of the world. Its source is in the streams that tumble down from the high Himalayas of northern India. It crosses the wide Indian plains, east and south, and flows into the Bay of Bengal below the city of Calcutta.

Since ancient times Indians have said that rivers, especially the Ganges River, came from the gods. To the Hindus, the Ganges is most holy at the point where it curves like a crescent moon. Here they have built hundreds of temples and their most sacred city, *Varanasi* (sometimes called Banaras).

In the gardens of the city and on the banks of the river, century after century, holy men have sat and meditated. Century after century, people have gone down into the river to bathe and pray. And always, through the years, beside the river the dead have been burned and

33

their ashes scattered on its sacred waters. All year, but especially in the festival seasons of October and November, pilgrims come to Varanasi. By foot, by bullock cart, by camel cart, horse cart, and, more recently, by train, they crowd in on Varanasi. Excitement rises as they near the wide Ganges River. They look at its waters with awe. Some throw in coins. The holy men look at it in reverence with palms together before their faces.

Those who come by train crowd to the windows. Pushing, hurrying, shouting, calling to one another, the people get off the train at Varanasi. Porters pick up the luggage and, carrying it on their heads, force a passage through the crowds. On the platform there is laughter, shouting, and friendly conversation. Outside the station the horse carriages and cycle-rickshaws wait, their drivers trying to get the attention of the travelers. Then, loaded with passengers, the carriages and rickshaws race toward the inns near the river.

Along the road men sell flowers and incense, cymbals, beads, and images of the gods. On the pathway leading to the banks of the river the beggars sit—old men and women, lepers, the blind, the sick, asking the passer-by to be kind and give them alms.

Breathless with awe, the Hindu family arrives at the temples on the bank and hurries down the many steps to the river. They see Brahmin priests sitting under wide straw umbrellas. They go to the priest who, with his ancestors, has served their family for generations. They tell him every important event in the family since they last saw him, and he keeps it in their family record. They leave their outer garments with him and wade out into the water—the women and girls on one part of the bank, the men and boys on another. They lift the holy water of the river in cupped palms. They drink and gargle. They face the sun and join their palms before their faces and bow.

They wash their clothes, skillfully changing beside the water. They return to the priest who puts a spot of sandalwood paste on their foreheads. Now the family goes to visit the many temples.

In Varanasi, as in all India, the many temples have many images. There are temples with images of many gods and goddesses. There are temples with images of the red monkey-god, *Hanuman*. There are temples with images of the elephant-headed god, *Ganesh*. There are images of bulls. There are images of dancing gods with many arms, and of gods sitting cross-legged like holy men. There are temples with frightening goddesses, all white or pitch black.

In these temples and before these idols, Hindus worship. A Brahmin priest might explain that all idols represent God whom no one can know. And because no one can know God, there are many ways of thinking about God and worshipping God.

Many Ways

There are many patterns of religion among the Hindus. There is the way of sacrifice and the way of penance. There are the ways of meditation and of religious acts, and of devotion.

The earliest pattern was the way of *yajña* or "sacrifice"—of giving gifts to the gods and flattering them to win their favour. Many Hindus still follow this way.

There was the way of the holy men or hermits who left their homes to live simply and to endure hardships (*tapas* or "austerity") in mountains, forests, or even in the crowded city streets. Some lived by themselves. Others came together in hermitages in the forest and studied the book, *Thoughts for Forest Men*. Hindus still admire men who give up everything to spend their time meditating and concentrating on the meaning of life.

There was the way of asking questions and finding answers. The holy men asked such questions as: "Who are we?" "What is real, and what is unreal?" "How do we get away from trouble in this world?" People who stayed at home also talked about these questions with their friends. Most of the men who asked these questions were Brahmins. Some, however, belonged to the caste of princes and warriors.

Thinkers

The men who asked questions tried to find answers. "Are you always punished when you do wrong?" was one of the questions they tried to answer. It had been said, "Anyone who does wrong suffers for it. Those who do right are rewarded."

"But," argued the *thinkers*, "it does not always turn out that way. We all know good people who suffer. Sometimes it seems that the good suffer, and the bad prosper."

Finally most thinkers agreed that people either pay for or are rewarded for the deeds they do. Those who lead a miserable existence in this life are paying for the wrongs they did in a previous existence. Those who are born into a happy life are being rewarded for the good they did in a former life.

"But what if someone who is paying in this life for a bad previous life keeps on doing wrong?" asked some.

"In that case," said the thinkers, "he will have to be born again into a still more miserable existence."

The thinkers agreed this could go on for eight million four hundred thousand births and rebirths. They said every act a person does must be rewarded or punished. At death the good and bad a person has done determine his next life. The Hindus call this *karma* or the "law of deeds." He who continues to do bad things will, in each life, be born as something worse: a slave, an insect, or even a dog. (Hindus do not think much of dogs.) He who continues to live a good life may be reborn into a prosperous family, or as a prince, or, even better, as a priest. Better yet, he may be born as a cow, an animal sacred to the Hindus. This living over and over again is called *transmigration*.

Life at its best, however, is full of trouble. So Indian thinkers felt that the finest thing that could happen to anyone was not to be born over again. But how could one escape rebirth, if everything one does has to be paid for in another life on earth? Obviously, it seemed, the only way to escape being reborn was to do nothing. But how can one exist doing nothing?

Men who thought about these problems could be found in India as long ago as 650 B.C. and for many centuries after that. They were sometimes called *Ford-finders*. In the days of no bridges, Ford-finders were men who found the best places to cross rivers. "Existence," said many thinkers, "is like a wide river. It takes many lifetimes to cross this river." Religious Ford-finders were men who tried to find ways to cross over existence to the opposite side so that they would not have to be born again.

Conquerors

There was one thinker, or Ford-finder, who felt he had found the secret of getting rid of existence, of doing away with having to be born over and over again. His friends called him *Mahavira*—"the Great Hero," or *Jina*—"the Conqueror." He did not look like a hero or a conqueror. He was thin and scrawny, lived simply, and had no army with which to conquer anything or anyone. An old proverb says, "He who conquers himself, conquers the world." Mahavira's followers said, "He has conquered himself."

Mahavira, they said, was not like most people in whom a good conscience and bad desires are always at war. Mahavira was different. He no longer wanted to do anything wrong. He was never angry, not even at the mosquitoes that bit him. He was never hungry or thirsty although he ate and drank little. He was never unhappy. What was his secret?

He told his friends his secret. The secret, he said, was to deny himself the things most people want until he no longer wanted them. He told them they could get rid of existence by eating as little as possible, owning as few possessions as possible, refraining from drinking intoxicating beverages or eating meat or telling lies or talking foolishly. He said that Spirit lives in everything—in people, in animals, in insects,

RELIGIONS AROUND THE WORLD

even in grains of dust. He told his followers, "Never kill or harm any creature. Never eat food prepared especially for you, for that would mean that some kind of life has been destroyed just so you can exist." Mahavira and his friends wore shoes with pointed spike heels so that they would step on as little ground as possible when they walked and thus avoid crushing insects. With a soft broom they swept the ground in front of them as they went along to brush insects out of the way. They wore thin cloth masks over their mouths to keep from swallowing insects.

Mahavira lived from 599-527 B.C. Those who believed as he did and followed his way called themselves *Jains* or "Conquerors." There are still many Jains in India today who keep the religion of Mahavira. They have beautiful temples with no idols but with many statues of famous Ford-finders. Their religion teaches them to be an industrious hard-working people. They have always laid much stress on strict simplicity in their living.

Enlightened One

When Mahavira was an old man, another Ford-finder came along who felt that he had discovered the key to getting rid of existence. His name was *Gautama*. He told his friends that existence and suffering come as a result of desiring things. He told them to stop wanting things, stop caring about what happens, stop imagining they were anybody. He told them to forget themselves and live a practical life of goodness. Then, he said, there would be an end to troubled existence.

People called Gautama the *Buddha*, which means "the Enlightened One." Those who followed him were called *Buddhists*. Buddhism grew to become one of the important religions of the world. (See Chapter 4.)

Books for Sitting Down and Thinking

Many books were written by Hindu thinkers.

Most thinkers did not leave the Hindu religion as did Mahavira the Jain, and Gautama the Buddha. They simply added their ideas to Hinduism. Their ideas were written down in the *Upanishads* which is a short name for "Sitting at the feet of a teacher and listening to him explain the secret knowledge of the holy books, the Vedas."

Upanishads were sometimes written in the form of a conversation. One of their stories tells of a king who asked his court Brahmins questions that they could not answer. They could tell the king how to carry out sacrifices to the gods. They could tell him how to govern his country. But they could not answer his main questions, "What is real?" "Who am I?" "Who are you?" So the king gave his own answers.

The most famous answer in the Upanishads is to the question, "Who are you?" The answer is, "You are *That!*" It sounds like a riddle, and it is a riddle. The meaning of the riddle is found in the explanation of *That. That,* say the Hindu thinkers, is something greater than anything anyone can imagine or describe. *That* is greater than the gods. It is everything that is really real. It is not the earth and the sun, and the trees, and the animals you see, but it is the real part of all of them.

Are you the things you wear? No. Are you the things you eat? No. Are you your age? No. Are you your feet? Your arms? No. Are you your face? No. There is something real in you, but you cannot explain it. You know it is there, however. Maybe you call it your *Self.* There is a Self in everybody. The Hindus call this Self the *Atman.* It is like the breath you breathe. You cannot see your breath (except, you say, on a cold day). Yet, you could not live without breath. Everybody lives by breath. Breath is really the same in everybody. Everybody has a Self and Self is really the same in everybody. That is the important conclusion to which the Hindu thinkers came.

Said one thinker: "We are like the water in cups on a table. You pour the water into all the cups from the same pitcher. There are many kinds of cups, but the water is the same in all of them. We, like the water, are really all the same."

Said another thinker: "We are like drops of water in the ocean. There are millions of drops, all part of the ocean. There are millions of people in the world, all part of the same thing."

One writer explained it this way: A father said to his son, "Here is salt. Put it in a cup of water. Then come and bring it to me tomorrow morning."

The next morning the father commanded his son, "Give me back the salt you put in the water yesterday." The son could not find the salt. It had dissolved.

So the father said, "Taste the surface of the water. How is it?"

The son tasted it and replied, "It is salty."

"Pour a little out and taste it from the middle of the cup," said the father. "How is it?"

The son tasted and again replied, "It is salty."

"Now pour the rest of it out and taste it from the bottom. How is it?"

"It is salty," said the son.

The father explained, "The salt you cannot see. You cannot separate it from the water. It is not water. Yet, it is all through the water. Like the unseen salt that is all through the water, there is an unseen *something* that is in all of us. We look and act differently from each other. Each of us changes a little from day to day. Yet, there is *something* in each of us that is the same and it never changes. It is *That*."

The Hindus call *That* by the name *Brahman*. The name looks like the word Brahmin but it is not the same word. That is why it is spelled differently in this book. It should be pronounced differently, too. The Brahmin priest is pronounced *BRAH-muhn*. The Brahman which is *That* is pronounced *BRUH-muhn*.

Brahman is real, the Hindu teachers said. Brahman cannot be seen or distinguished. On the other hand, those things which we can see or distinguish are not real. We are confused when we think they are real. This confusion the Hindu teachers called *Maya*.

"It is *Maya* that causes all the trouble," the Hindu thinkers said. "We think we are real all by ourselves. We think we are different from one another. We become attached to people and to things. This attachment to the world makes it necessary for us to be born over and over again."

"Is there any way out of this continuous troubled existence?" people asked. The thinkers said there were two ways out. "The first," they explained, "is the way of *jñana,* or 'realizing.' Stop your activity. Stop caring about things and people. Get off by yourselves and meditate. Concentrate on *That,* on Brahman. Think about nothing else."

It may take years, or even lifetimes, of practice. This practice of self-control is called *yoga.* He who practises yoga (called a *yogi*) first learns to control his body—breath, muscles, and limbs. Next he learns to control his mind so that he can concentrate. Finally, through concentration, he comes to realize that he and Brahman are the same. When this happens he will cease being born over and over again.

The second way out, according to the thinkers, was the way of *karma,* "doing." Doing is not so hard as realizing. The thinkers said, "Carry out the religious practices demanded by the priests. Do them as well as you can. Fulfil all the obligations of your caste. Stop caring about anything. Perhaps, then, when you die you will not have to be born over again. Or, if you must be born over again, it could be that you will be born to become a holy man. When you are a holy man, you can practise the way of realizing."

More is said about this in India's most famous scripture, the *Bhagavad Gita,* the "Song of the Lord." The Bhagavad Gita tells of Krishna who, as a chariot driver, advised a prince about to go unwillingly into battle. Prince Arjuna did not want to fight. Relatives, friends, and men he respected were in the enemy army and he did not want to kill them. Krishna, the driver of his chariot, however, urged him into the battle. He told the prince it was his duty as a warrior to fight, that unhappiness comes from caring too much about people and things. Unhappiness, the chariot-driver explained, is brought about by anger and greed, by hating and loving. He advised, "Do your duty as a prince and as a warrior. Fight without hating or loving."

Krishna said that everyone should do his work well, whatever it is, without caring about the results of his work. He said people should keep their minds fixed on worshipping God. This, according to the Bhagavad Gita, is the third way out. It is the way of *bhakti*, "adoration." Anyone—not just the wise and holy men—can follow this way. Krishna, who the Bhagavad Gita said was really the great, unknowable God *That,* in human form, advised, "Adore me, as God. Put all your thoughts on me. Love me. Worship me. And I will save you."

Singing Saints

There were many Hindus who followed the way of adoration. They spent much of their time worshipping God in songs of love to him.

Hindus say that God, *That,* shows himself to the world in three forms.

The first is the form of God as creator. God created the world. The world is his idle act.

The second is the form of God as preserver. God preserves the world. He keeps it going.

The third is the form of God as destroyer. God destroys the world. It is like clearing the stage so that the play can begin over again.

Only God, *That,* which is in everything and everyone, is never created and never destroyed.

Brahma is the name of God as creator.

Vishnu is the name of God as preserver.

Shiva is the name of God as destroyer.

All over India poets began to write and sing songs to one of these forms of God. The poets were the *singing saints* of India.

Not many wrote about God as Brahma. Brahma had already created the world and was not so important in day-to-day life. From early times, however, and especially in South India, singing saints wrote songs to Shiva, the destroyer form of God. "Shiva," they sang, "is the

▲ Brahmin priest (Ceylon) prepares religious articles for ceremony in a Hindu temple.

▲ Effigies of Ravana and two other demons in the Ramlila play at a festival in India.

◄ The Golden Temple, most sacred shrine of the Sikhs (Amritsar, India).

real Brahman. He is the real God." In their poems they called Shiva "father," "mother," "lover," "friend." Their songs were love songs to Shiva. Songs the singing saints wrote to Shiva over a thousand years ago are still sung in India today.

Pictures of Shiva show him seated cross-legged on a tiger skin in meditation. He is the ancient hermit god. Ashes cover his long, often matted, hair and are smeared on his body. Nearby are his sacred white bull and his elephant-headed son. As the destroyer god he is shown as an emaciated, fearsome holy man, sometimes wearing a necklace of skulls. To his worshippers, however, he is beautiful. He only destroys the old in order that new life can take its place, they say. They tell a story about a deadly poison which Shiva drank. The poison had emerged out of the churned-up ocean and Shiva drank it to keep it from harming any creature.

There are stories about Shiva's wife who appears in the forms of many goddesses and is called by many different names. These goddesses represent Shiva's energy. Hindus believe that Shiva's energy is given to those who worship these goddesses.

From early times, and especially from the twelfth to the eighteenth century in North India, singing saints wrote songs to Vishnu, the preserving form of God. They thought of Vishnu as Brahman. In Vishnu, they said, we see his love for his worshippers. He watches over them from the skies and protects them. Although Vishnu is as far away as the sun is far from the earth, nevertheless, he comes to his worshippers now and then. He comes to them, they declared, when they pray to him and beg him to come. Sometimes he appears to them in a vision.

Vishnu is mentioned in the ancient Vedas. He was the sun god. Hindu pictures of Vishnu show him with a crown of light on his head, a halo which is the sun. He has four arms and hands. In one hand he holds a royal mace. In another he holds a discus, his powerful weapon. In his other two hands he holds a conch shell and a lotus flower. He rides through the skies on an eagle. As the preserver God, Vishnu is pictured as a handsome, healthy young man. He has a smile for his worshippers and is kind and generous, they say.

There are stories about Vishnu's wife, *Lakshmi,* who is also called *Shri.* She is the symbol of prosperity. Businessmen honour her each morning so that they will have good business all day long.

God Among the People

Vishnu, the Hindus say, has come to earth from time to time to restore the worship of the gods when human beings have become careless about their religion. He comes in the disguise of an animal or of a man to destroy evil in the world. There are stories of his coming as a tortoise, as a fish, as a man-lion, as a boar, as a dwarf, and as a terrible-tempered Brahmin who fought with an axe. He came once as Rama, the hero prince, and once as Krishna, the cowkeeper. These appearances of Vishnu are called *Avatara,* "descents."

Rama was an ancient hero-king. Pictures show him carrying a bow which once belonged to the god Shiva. Rama alone had been strong enough to lift it. With it he could hit any target from a great distance. Rama was strong in battle and wise in governing his subjects.

No one can understand Brahman, the great *That.* Rama they can understand, so they worship God as Rama. Rama represents Brahman. Rama, they say, was born and grew up as a prince in order to bring about an orderly world based on religion. When anyone worships Rama he also respects people in the higher castes such as Brahmins and rulers. Like Rama he becomes kind and generous to people in the lower castes and to servants.

The story of Rama as Vishnu in disguise is a popular scripture in India called the *Ramayana.* It says that Rama, when he was on earth, saved anyone who called on him. The meanest criminal who called out Rama's name was sure of his help. Rama saves anyone from being punished in another life for what he has done in this life. Rama takes him to his gardens in heaven where he can live happily.

In fields and orchards and along the roadsides of India are shrines to Rama where passers-by may stop and pray. In the shrines can be seen the red image of Rama, of his wife Sita, and their friend the red monkey-god, Hanuman.

Krishna, in Hindu stories, was a playfully mischievous cowherd. Pictures of Krishna are everywhere in India—on calendars, on dishes, and on the walls of shops, schools, and homes. He is usually shown playing his flute. With his flute he made music for his girl friends while he herded cows.

No one can understand Brahman, the great *That*. Krishna they can understand, so they worship God as Krishna. Krishna represents Brahman. Krishna's girl friends represent his worshipers.

Other stories about Krishna describe the great strength he displayed when, as a youth, he killed millions of demons. These stories, Hindus say, show that God, Krishna, came in human form to destroy evil and to bring to his heaven those who worship him.

Krishna is especially popular with boys and girls and young people in the schools and colleges of India.

For sixteen hundred years the worship of Shiva and of Rama and Krishna has been a popular, joyful, singing form of religion. The people of India love to tell and to listen to stories about these gods, their wives, friends, and faithful worshippers. They love to sing together songs of praise to them. In return, they say, God is generous and kind to all who call on him and will save them to his heaven. Some Hindus have said that all God's power is in the name by which he is called, so that anyone repeating the name Rama, for example, would be saved in heaven just for repeating the name. This religion of bhakti means not only to adore God, but to live together in respect and kindness in the world. It means to respect holy men and Brahmins and everybody who has a superior position in society, for every superior person, in a way, represents God. On the other hand, it means that everyone should be kind and generous to anyone who comes and asks for help and anyone who serves in an inferior position. In a way, everyone must act like God to those who are dependent on him. Some teachers have said that all worshippers are equal in God's sight, and therefore caste differences mean nothing in worship.

Learners

Nanak (1469-1538) lived in the Punjab in North India at a time when India was ruled by Muslim conquerors from Persia. He saw that the Hindu gods had not been able to keep the Muslims out. He heard that the Muslims believed, not in many gods or images of God, but in one, unseen God. They made no pictures or idols of their God.

As a boy, Nanak often thought about God and wondered what he was really like. "We Hindus have so many idols I sometimes get confused," he said. "Maybe the Muslims are right."

Nanak listened to the poems and songs of Kabir, one of India's greatest poets. The poet Kabir said that to repeat some name of God over and over, as many Hindus did, was silly, and to perform religious rites was worthless. He taught that idols are not gods and do not represent God. He said the stories about many of the gods are untrue. The true unseen God, he wrote, has nothing to do with such foolishness. What God wants in people is cleanness of heart.

Nanak, when he grew up, thought more and more about God and often composed his own songs in praise of God. One day he dreamed that God came to him and said, "Tell people everywhere to revere my name, to think about me, to live clean lives."

This led Nanak to travel to many parts of India preaching against idol worship and against the caste system of the Hindus. He said, "There is only one God and all people are the same before God. In God's sight there are no castes, no Hindus, no Muslims. God wants you to revere his name and live a good life. If you do this, when you die instead of being born over again you will remain forever with God. God," he declared, "is in all of us. All God wants is true worshippers."

Many Muslims and Hindus thought Nanak's teachings made good sense. They followed him and called him their *guru,* that is, their "teacher." They called themselves *Sikhs* or "learners."

When Nanak died another teacher took his place. Each teacher was succeeded by another until a century and a half later, in 1675, *Gobind Rai* became the guru. By that time the Hindus and the Sikhs were rebelling against the harshness of their Muslim rulers. Many of the Sikhs had turned into fighters. Gobind Rai changed his name to *Gobind Singh* —"Gobind, the Lion." Every Sikh young man who followed Gobind Singh was baptized and took the name Singh. He was to be brave as a lion. He was never to cut his hair or beard, and he was always to carry a sword.

Ever since then, most Sikhs have not cut their hair or beards. They wear tight turbans to keep their hair in place. They are intelligent, hard-working people. They are soldiers, businessmen, and scientists. They have their own scripture called the *Granth.* This is a collection of the hymns of their gurus. In their temples there are no idols, only the Granth. Congregations gather to hear the reading of the Granth and listen to sermons from it. Today there are Sikhs in many parts of the world as well as in India.

Remakers

The Sikhs or "learners" were remakers of Hinduism. They wanted to bring new thoughts to Hinduism. By the 18th century Sikhism was a well-established religion in India.

In the 19th century many Europeans, especially the British, came to India and brought new ideas.

In the city of Calcutta, *Ram Mohan Rai* was one of the Indians who studied the new ideas brought from Europe. He also studied other religions. Some of his ideas about religion came from his Protestant Christian friends. He wanted Hindus to give up idols, to direct their minds to the one unseen God alone, to keep a high code of conduct in their relations with each other. He said no one is ever born over and over again, and no one becomes part of God. Ram Mohan Rai held meetings in which he and his friends talked about the great teachings of many religions, including the teachings of Jesus. They called their society the *Brahma Samaj*, the "Society of God."

More popular is the Arya Samaj, the "Society of the Noble." *Dayanand Sarasvati* started it in 1875. He said that Hinduism's earliest hymns, the Vedas, contained all that was best for religion. In the ancient days of the Vedas there had been no idols and no castes. People had worshipped God with a fire that had burned their offerings. Satyavati said, "Let us get back to the Hinduism of our Aryan ancestors who came over the mountains into India." Members of the Arya Samaj worship God simply, making fire the centre of their worship. They say, "God is clean and bright like a fire." The Arya Samaj is not only trying to remake Hinduism into what its members say Hinduism was in early times, they are also trying to keep other religions, such as Christianity and Islam, out of India. Today, in India, many belong to the Arya Samaj.

Ramakrishna (1834-1886) was a different kind of remaker. He was priest in the temple of the goddess *Kali* in Calcutta. One night he dreamed that Kali came and thanked him for being her priest. On other nights he dreamed that Rama and Krishna, the gods for whom he was named, came and talked with him. He dreamed that the Buddha, the Lord of Buddhism, and Jesus, the Lord of Christianity, visited him in the same way. He worshipped and praised them all. He decided they were all forms of the same God. He said, "You can go into a temple from many sides by different steps. Inside, however, you find the same altar and the same idol in the centre of the temple. The many religions of the world are like that. They go by different ways, but they are all seeking Truth."

Ramakrishna had many followers. The best known of his followers was *Vivekananda*. He went around the world lecturing on the teachings

49

of Ramakrishna. He said that all religions are much alike, that they say the same thing in many different ways, but that the Hindu way is the most sensible. In India he started the Ramakrishna missions to help people in need. He formed an order of Hindu monks to run the missions. He patterned the missions after the Christian missions he had seen. They include schools, hospitals, and community centres. The Ramakrishna Mission publishes books, magazines, poems, and tracts that explain the meaning of Hinduism.

Hindu Festivals

A religious festival can be found going on some place in India at any time of the year, for every temple has at least one festival to honour its principal god.

Among the most popular festivals are *Holi, Dasera,* and *Divali.*

Holi is a gay festival celebrated at the beginning of spring. People delight in squirting coloured water on each other and on passers-by. Effigies, representing the demons Krishna is said to have killed, are burned in huge bonfires.

Dasera, a ten-day festival, celebrates Rama's battle against Ravana. In parts of India it comes at the same time as the worship of a goddess sometimes called *Durga.* Durga is worshipped with great pomp and parades. On the tenth day, in many towns throughout India, a play is staged portraying the battle between Rama and Ravana. The play ends when Rama shoots arrows into a huge effigy of Ravana filled with firecrackers, and it explodes and burns.

Divali, the feast of lights, is a four-day festival that comes in October or November and celebrates the new year. Homes are given a thorough cleaning and outlined with tiny clay lamps to welcome into the home *Lakshmi,* the goddess of prosperity. Firecrackers are set off to frighten away evil spirits, businessmen open new account books, and everyone eats sweets and cakes.

Hindus Today

Along the rivers of India and in the temples, many Hindus practise their religion as it has been practised for thousands of years. In fact, there is a revival of ancient forms of Hindu worship. In the great changes that are taking place in India, many people find comfort in the religion that their ancestors followed. More than ever, individuals stop to worship at shrines. Great crowds gather at religious festivals. Groups sing and march around booths where there are pictures of their gods, or they parade in procession behind the image of a favourite goddess. On special occasions they gather to sing hymns all night. Some meet regularly to recite in responsive fashion their holy texts and to listen as a teacher explains their meaning.

Other Hindus are studying the writings of the ancient Hindu thinkers. They quote the great scriptures of Hinduism, especially the Bhagavad Gita. They are putting new ideas into the old words. Many of these new ideas have come to them from modern sciences and from other religions, especially from Christianity. These people are often called *neo-Hindus*, "new-Hindus." Many of these new-Hindus call for goodwill among men. They urge Hindus to believe in the new religious teachings and to live unselfishly. In the twentieth century, Mohandas Gandhi (1869-1948) used the Hindu Bhagavad Gita to teach self-forgetfulness. He also lived by the teachings of the Sermon on the Mount found in the Christian New Testament.

For Hindus, religion may take many forms. Because most Hindus believe that God is the something real in all the world and in every person, they consider that good religion is to look beyond the things that change and die to a truth that is unchanging. That truth, they say, is untouched by human fear or by human love. It is unmoved by anything that happens. No one can explain it. No one can imagine it. Yet, Hindus say, when people respect each other and worship any deity of any name in any religion, they are trying to get to this truth.

51

IV
Buddhism

An Unhappy Prince

Among the snow-topped Himalayan Mountains, to the north east of India, lies the mountain kingdom of Nepal. Here, on the border of India, in 560 B.C. *Siddhartha Gautama* was born. His father was a prince, a member of the Hindu warrior caste. He gave Gautama everything to make him happy—friends, servants, fine clothes, good food, games, and entertainment. Gautama played in the gardens that surrounded his house. His father had been told that if he could keep his son from knowing the miseries of life, the prince some day would be ruler of all India. The father commanded his friends and servants, "Be sure that Siddhartha sees nothing that is ugly or unpleasant." When the prince went for a ride in his chariot, servants went ahead to clear the road of beggars and sick and old people. Gautama grew up believing there was no trouble in the world. He thought everyone was happy, healthy, and lived forever. Yet, Gautama himself was not happy.

When Gautama was sixteen his father arranged his marriage to a beautiful princess. In time a son was born to Gautama and his princess. But still Gautama was not happy.

53

Riding one day in the country, the story says, Gautama's chariot passed a feeble old man leaning on a cane. "What is the matter with him?" Gautama asked the driver. "He is old," said the driver. "Once he was young, but now he has grown old." So the prince learned that people do not stay young forever.

The chariot passed a beggar full of sores, lying by the side of the road. "What is the matter with him?" asked Gautama. "He is sick," said the driver. "Once he was healthy, but now he is sick." So Gautama learned there is sickness and disease in the world.

They passed four men carrying a corpse. "What is the matter with him?" asked Gautama. "He is dead," said the driver. "Yesterday he was alive, but today he is dead." So Gautama learned about death.

Gautama went home to think about what he had seen. He asked himself, "Why do people get old, get sick, and die?" The thought struck him, "I, too, may someday grow old, get sick, and die."

Later, as he sat in his garden thinking, Gautama saw coming down the road a holy man dressed in a simple yellow robe. He seemed peaceful and contented. Gautama thought, "I would rather be like that holy man than have all the games and food and the clothes and the good times of my father's house."

Gautama's father tried to make his son happy. He arranged gay parties for him with his friends. One night he brought dancers to the palace to dance for them. The guests ate and drank and laughed and talked and at last fell asleep where they were. Gautama, however, did not eat and drink, and he did not sleep. He thought, "How silly all this is. Tomorrow everyone will be tired and a little older, and that is all. It doesn't mean a thing."

Gautama made a decision. He kissed his sleeping wife and baby boy. He called his servant. "Get our horses ready," he ordered. "We are going for a ride." The two of them rode through the dark night until they reached the river border of his father's land. They crossed the river. There Gautama dismounted. He shaved his black hair. He took off his jewels and princely clothes and put on the coarse yellow robe of a hermit holy man. He gave his jewels and clothes, his sword and horse to his servant. "Take these back to my father's house," he said. "I do not need them anymore."

Gautama's Search

Gautama went into the forest.

First, he went to a hill where hermits lived in caves. The hermits were Brahmin Hindu philosophers. Gautama asked them why there is so much trouble in the world. He asked them to teach him how to escape forever this miserable existence of suffering. The philosophers said, "Practise yoga, the control of your body, your muscles, your breath. Think the way we think and meditate on *That,* the God, Brahman-atman, until at last your mind is empty of all thoughts. Then you will not have to be born over and over again into this world of suffering."

Gautama practised yoga. He learned what the Brahmins taught him. He thought quietly about *That* for a long time. Then he said to the Brahmins, "Nothing you say makes good sense to me. You are just using big words. For all I know, even *That,* the God, Brahman-atman, is just a big word." Gautama left the Brahmins.

Next, he looked for hermit holy men who would not talk nonsense, but would act with good sense. He found in the forests some of the followers of Mahavira, the Conqueror, who had conquered himself. They lived quiet simple lives. They talked little. They ate little and wore few clothes. Gautama asked them why there is so much trouble in the world. He asked them to teach him how to escape forever this miserable existence of suffering. The hermits said, "Go hungry, wear little, say little, empty your mind of all thoughts. Live a hard, honest life as we do and do not disturb the bugs that crawl on your body. Then you will not have to be born over and over again into this world of suffering."

Gautama did what they told him. He ate little and soon resembled a skeleton. He washed so little he soon itched all over. By night he slept on thorns. By day he stood for hours in one position without moving. He soon became famous for what he could endure. He lived like this for six years. People said, "He is a great holy man. He can endure more than any other holy man." Yet, Gautama realized that his mind, instead of becoming more clear became dull through weakness, so dull he could not work out the answers to his questions.

At last Gautama said, "This, too, does not make sense. I must eat and exercise, or I cannot think." He began to eat and to sleep on the ground. The hermits were shocked. So Gautama left them.

Gautama went to sit by himself under a pipal tree in the forest. For a long time he thought. At last, one day, like a flash of light, the answers to his questions came. "Now I understand," he said to himself. "I must ignore myself. I must stop wanting things. I must even stop caring about life. I must be helpful to others who are looking for escape from this troubled existence." Gautama realized he no longer cared about himself or about life. He was happy at last.

Gautama decided to share his discovery with his former hermit friends. He found them sitting together in the Deer Park near the Hindu holy city of Varanasi. It was night, but a full moon was shining. The five hermits saw Gautama and said to each other, "Here comes the fellow who went back to the soft life. Let us pay no attention to him." As Gautama drew nearer, however, by the light of the moon they saw his face. It was peaceful and contented. They decided to listen to what he had to say. Gautama sat down among them.

In the Deer Park

"I have found the way," Gautama said.

"What way?" the holy men asked.

"We have been on the wrong path. We have been abusing ourselves, making ourselves sick. This does no good. It is painful, and it makes the mind dull. On the other hand a comfortable life is vulgar and stupid, and it, too, makes the mind dull."

"Then what is the way you have found?" asked the hermits.

"It is the *Middle Way,*" explained Gautama. "Avoid both extremes. Don't indulge yourself. Don't overeat. Don't drink. Don't make a fool of yourself by trying to have a good time.

"On the other hand, don't starve yourself, either. Don't go without sleep. Don't look for hardship. Follow the Middle Way and your mind will be clear and sharp.

"Religious ceremonies and the worship of idols are foolishness. So is praying to God. What good does it do? No good! There may be many gods, but they are no better off than we. We do not know any God who can help us."

Years later, Buddhist teachers said that Gautama had also declared, "We don't even know if we have any selves." But that was philosophy, and he was not interested in philosophy. "Philosophy," he said, "is just piling up guesses. All I know is that I find myself in a troubled world, and I have to find some practical way to live in it."

"What is the way you have found?" asked the hermits.

"Be honest in everything you do," said Gautama. "Be kind to others. Forget yourself. Most important: stop wanting things for yourself.

"My way is based on four sensible ideas that came to me while I was thinking under a tree in the forest. They are four facts we must understand if we are to live in this world."

These four sensible ideas Buddhists call *Four Noble Truths.*

Four Noble Truths

1. There is the *noble truth of suffering.* Life is full of suffering. It is painful to be born. It is painful to grow old. It is painful to be sick and to die. It is painful to be annoyed. It is painful not to get what we want. It is painful when people we love and things we like are taken from us. Just to exist is painful. Life is full of misery and suffering.

2. There is the *noble truth of the cause of suffering*. Life is full of suffering because we are always wanting things. Wanting things causes us to be born over and over again. Life is wanting pleasure. It is wanting to exist. It is wanting prosperity. We want what we do not have. We want to hold on to what we do have. Governments go to war to defend what they have or to get what they think they should have. Wanting things always causes suffering.

3. There is the *noble truth of the way to stop suffering*. Pain and suffering disappear when we stop wanting things. When we no longer want anything, when we are free from desire, we stop suffering.

4. There is the *noble truth of the way which leads to the end of suffering*. This way has eight steps. Gautama said his eight steps would take away all desire to have things and thus free a person from suffering.

The Eight-Step Path

The *eight-step path* is the path to peacefulness. The steps are not easy steps. They are like large steps up a hill.

Step one is *right belief*. Believe the four noble truths. Admit that life is full of suffering, and the only way to put an end to suffering is to stop wanting.

Step two is *right purpose*. Want nothing for yourself. Want nothing that will make others suffer.

Step three is *right speech*. Speak sensibly without hurting anyone. Do not speak foolish things. Say no cross words. Say nothing against anyone. Speak only words that are helpful.

Step four is *right conduct*. Behave with goodwill for all. Be kind to everyone and everything.

Step five is *right means of livelihood*. Use your time and energy in a way that will harm no one. Do not earn your living in a way that causes misery to any living creature.

Step six is *right effort*. Keep your mind alert to choose between what is good and what is not good.

Step seven is *right concentration*. Concentrate on what is useful. Do not let your mind wander.

Step eight is *right enjoyment*. At last your life will be calm and contented, passing, at death, into quiet peace. Step eight is the top of the hill.

The Beginning of Trouble

Trouble begins with ourselves.

"Nothing will bother you," said Gautama, "unless you yourself let it bother you."

"No one and no thing outside ourselves," explained Gautama, "can make us happy. Owning things does not make us happy. Trying to be like others does not make us happy. Happiness comes only when we make up our minds to live in the right way. The trouble is with ourselves," he said. "We think too much of ourselves."

"Who are we anyway?" Buddhists answer that question with another question: "What is a chariot?" The answer is that a chariot is a combination of wheels and axles, shaft, and carriage. Take the parts of the chariot away, and there is no chariot. "You are like that," say Buddhists. "You are a combination of your body, your feelings, your understanding, your instincts, your thoughts. Take these away and there is no 'you' left. Even these parts of you change each year. Each day you are really not quite the same person you were the day before. No one and no things are worth fighting over. After a few years you will outgrow and forget whatever you now think is important. At last you will die and disappear altogether. You see, you are not very important. No one is." This is what many Buddhists have taught.

Buddhists, like Hindus, say that people are born over and over again into this world after they die. But many Buddhists add, "It really is not we who are born over again, but it is the things we do, the way we feel, and our desire to live. These are born over again. When we do wrong, then our wrong deeds and wishes and feelings have to be born over again. But when we stop doing wrong, stop wanting things, stop having feelings, then there is nothing left to be born over again. Then we are like lamps that stop burning when there is no fuel."

The Buddha and His Companions

For several days Gautama and the hermits talked together in the Deer Park. The hermits were impressed. Gautama and they had been in the dark groping for a way out of this troubled existence. Now Gautama had discovered the way in his simple eight-step path. He had been enlightened. So they called him the *Buddha* which means "the Enlightened One."

The Buddha and his friends went about their country preaching the Four Noble Truths. Many who heard their preaching followed them. Some of Gautama's relatives joined his company. His cousin *Ananda* became his most devoted and intimate companion. Together Gautama and his followers built a few small huts in a grove of trees. Here they lived simply. Word of the Buddha's Middle Way spread and people came to the grove to learn from him. Men shaved off their hair and beards to be like the Buddha. They gave up everything they owned and became monks. Each kept only three coarse yellow robes to dress in, a razor to shave with, a needle for mending the robe, and a begging bowl. Every morning they took their begging bowls and went to the village to beg for food. They ate whatever was given to them. And if nothing was given they did not complain, and they did not eat. They spent much of their time in meditation.

Women asked and received permission to stay in the grove. They shaved their heads and their eyebrows and became nuns.

The groups of monks and nuns were called the *Sangha* which means "the company." Those who joined the Sangha took three vows. Each said:

1. "I take refuge in the *Buddha,* the Enlightened One." This was a promise to follow the Buddha and accept his teachings.

2. "I take refuge in the *Dharma,* the teaching of the truth and the rules of the Sangha." This was a promise to obey the way of life taught by the Buddha.

3. "I take refuge in the *Sangha.*" This was a promise not to live any longer for oneself but with the monks or nuns according to the rules made by the Sangha.

For nearly 2500 years Buddhist monks and nuns have taken these vows. They still do.

Busy Monks

The Buddha and his monks were men with a mission. During the nine dry months of the year they travelled in many parts of north and east India. No matter where they were, in city or village, each morning they presented their begging bowls for people to fill. When noon came they ate. They went among the people and told all who would listen of the Middle Way of the Buddha. They were like men who had found their way out of a burning house and were telling others how to get out. "The world is burning up with troubles and quarrels and selfishness," they said, "because people are bent on getting things for themselves. It is all useless. Leave everything! Forget yourselves! Live a life of kindness, and you will find the way out of all the misery of life."

During the three rainy months each year the Buddha and his companions returned to their grove to study and to think together.

Deeds and Happiness

"You become what you do," say the Buddhists.

One day the Buddha, teaching near a Hindu temple, said to the crowd gathered around him, "The priests say that by bathing in the river, honouring idols, and meditating on *That,* the God, Brahman-atman, you can save yourselves from being born again into another miserable existence. This is foolishness. When we die we will not be the same persons we are now. We are always changing. We are always

▲ Couple worshipping before a shrine near the Shwedagon in Rangoon, Burma.

▼ Buddhist nun in meditation (Burma).

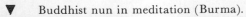

▲ A Burmese family before a reclining Buddha.

becoming what we do. If an honest person tells a lie and keeps on lying, he becomes a liar. If a sober person takes a drink and keeps on drinking, he becomes a drunkard. A person who lives unselfishly forgets himself. When he forgets himself he stops becoming anything because nothing bothers him. At this point he arrives at *Nirvana*."

But what is Nirvana? Many Buddhists think of it as a kind of heaven. The Buddhist teachers will not tell. They say they do not know. They say Nirvana is like a lamp going out when there is no more oil to keep it burning. It is like an electric light going out when the current is cut off. It is the end of suffering and trouble when one no longer cares about anything in the world.

Once a farmer saw the Buddha begging and said to him, "You say everyone should stop wanting things. But if everyone did stop wanting things no one would work. Then how would people eat? You beggars stay alive because we, who work, feed you."

The Buddha answered, "If everyone stopped wanting things no one would work for himself. Instead, people would help each other. Soon everyone would reach Nirvana, and then there would be no more struggle for existence and no more suffering."

Another time the Buddha told a crowd in a city, "When people try to hurt you they really only hurt themselves. Do not hit back. Pity their miserable existence." A man in the crowd decided to test the Buddha. He called him insulting names. The Buddha was silent.

"Aren't you going to answer me?" the man called out.

For answer the Buddha asked him a question, "If you give someone a gift but he does not accept it, to whom does the gift belong?" The man answered, "To him who offered it."

The Buddha said, "I do not take your insults. They belong to you."

The Buddha continued, "When anyone spits at the sky he doesn't dirty the sky. The spittle falls back on his own face. He who flings dust at another when the wind is blowing in his own direction only gets the dust back on himself."

The man looked ashamed. The next day he came to the Buddha and asked to be made one of his monks.

To Ceylon, Burma, and Beyond

More than two hundred years after the Buddha had died, a great warrior emperor, *Asoka,* ruled in India. He inherited a great empire from his grandfather and increased its size through the conquest of a neighbouring kingdom. His empire covered most of India.

Asoka did not feel proud of his conquest, however. "I cannot forget all the misery I have brought to my people," he would say. "Tens of thousands of soldiers have been killed! Many thousands of families are left without a father and a husband! Hundreds of towns and villages have been destroyed! And what for? For an empire which will fall to pieces some day as all empires do. And when I die, what good will my empire do me?"

One of his councillors remarked, "You sound like a Buddhist."

Asoka studied Buddhism. He came to believe the Buddhist way was the right way. He stopped all fighting. Inspired by Buddhist ideals, he engraved rules on rocks and on iron pillars which he erected in many parts of his empire. These ideals called on all people to live religious, orderly lives. They called on children to obey their parents, pupils to respect their teachers, everyone to be courteous in his relationships. They called on all to respect and care for living creatures, to avoid killing men and animals. They called for honesty, truth-speaking, and kindness as a way of life.

Asoka sent missionaries to all parts of India and to foreign countries to preach Buddhism. In Ceylon, missionaries built monasteries on forested mountaintops. In Burma they built a bell-shaped tower to remind people of the Buddha. In the Himalayas they preached to mountain people. In the west they talked with kings and princes. They urged all to follow the Buddha's way of peace. Asoka's monks converted thousands to Buddhism.

Three Baskets

For four hundred years the Buddhists had no book of scriptures. In the beginning the monks had learned from the Buddha or learned from each other what the Buddha had said.

When Gautama died, at the age of eighty, his friends feared his teachings would be lost. Buddhists say that one of his monks, Kassapa, had an idea. "We can keep all the Buddha's teachings from being lost," he said, "if we tell each other what each remembers." He called together five hundred Buddhist monks. They assembled at Rajagaha, the place where the Buddha used to meet them. They discussed together the teachings they remembered. Ananda, the Buddha's cousin, who had been with the Buddha at all times, listened to what the five hundred said. He added other teachings he had learned from the Buddha. This great body of teachings the monks memorized and kept in their minds by reciting them aloud. This meeting of the monks was called the First Buddhist Council.

The sayings of the Buddha were handed down by word of mouth for four hundred years. Then monks on the island of Ceylon gathered together all the teachings that anyone had ever heard and wrote them down. When they finished they had three books of nearly ten thousand pages. They called the three books the *Tripitaka,* or the "Three Baskets."

The first book was a collection of rules for Buddhist monks and nuns.

The second book was a collection of the Buddha's teachings.

The third book was a collection of comments about the Buddha's teachings.

The Three Baskets teach that real freedom is freedom from passion —from strong feelings and strong desires. They teach that when a person is free from wrong habits and wrong attitudes, then he is free from suffering and trouble.

The Three Baskets list rules to live by. Buddhists say anyone who follows these rules can be calm and happy. The rules say:

Do not kill.

Do not steal.

Do not go wrong with sensuous pleasure.

Do not lie.

Do not drink intoxicating beverages.

For monks and nuns there were additional and stricter rules. They were required to eat moderately, to dress simply, to sleep on pallets. They were to accept no gold or silver and were not to look at shows or dancing or listen to singing.

The Three Baskets are the scriptures of the Buddhists who live in southern Asia. Buddhists read them and memorize them to learn how to follow the way the Buddha taught.

Big Chariot, Little Chariot

There are different kinds of Buddhism.

Devadatta, a cousin of the Buddha, was a serious fellow. After Gautama's death he told the monks, "We must get up early. All morning we must beg, but all afternoon we must meditate. We must never eat anything after noon." People respected the monks.

Some monks, however, did not like the strict rules. They did not wish to have to arise so early in the morning. They wanted to eat in the afternoon if they were hungry. They saw no harm in wearing ornaments. They said to the strict ones, "You are riding a little chariot. Only a few can get on your chariot. Only a few can reach Nirvana in your Buddhism. It is only for the monks and nuns."

The not-so-strict monks started their own monasteries. They said, "We are riding a big chariot. There is room for all on our chariot. Everyone, not just monks and nuns who live by strict rules, can find a way to Nirvana or to heaven. Our Buddhism is for everybody. We are concerned not just for ourselves but for everyone."

The strict Buddhists call themselves *Theravadin,* "School of the Elders." The not-so-strict Buddhists call the strict Buddhists the *Hinayana,* or "little chariot" Buddhists. They call themselves the *Mahayana,* "big chariot" Buddhists.

The Mahayana Buddhists sent missionaries across the mountains to the north and all through northern Asia. They converted great numbers of people. Because they are found mostly in Asia north of India, they are called Northern Buddhists. The Hinayana Buddhists, who remained in southern Asia, are called Southern Buddhists.

Southern Buddhists

In the Deer Park near Varanasi are two temples built where Gautama the Buddha first explained his ideas to the hermits. One was built by Chinese Buddhists, a temple for Northern Buddhism. The other was built by the people of India, a temple for Southern Buddhism.

To these temples come people from all over the world, to worship and meditate. Southern Buddhists come from Ceylon, Burma, Thailand, and Cambodia in south east Asia. A few Indians come, too, but there are not many Buddhists in India,[1] the land of the Hindus.

In Ceylon, the Buddhist monasteries are places of quiet, far from the towns. There are many shrines for worship and many *stupas.* These are bell-shaped towers that hold remains of famous Buddhists monks, some say even of Gautama the Buddha. It is said that in one stupa there is a tooth of the Buddha. At sundown in Ceylon the sound of a bell calls people to worship. They come from their work, homes, and their schools. They come bringing candles and flowers to the temple.

In Burma there are stupas guarded by statues of a mythical dog-lion. The oldest stupa is the Shwe Dagon. In the Shwe Dagon, Burmese Buddhists say, are eight hairs from the Buddha's head, one hair for each of the eight steps in the eight-step path. The Shwe Dagon

[1] There was an increase in Indian Buddhism in the middle of the twentieth century.

is covered with gold and glitters in the sunshine. Around it are smaller stupas and small statues of the Buddha. Monks in yellow robes recite scriptures for those who do not themselves know how. When the recitations are finished a worshipper may place flowers at the feet of the Buddha's statue or pour cold water over it.

Almost every village and town has its monastery. Students are taught by the monks. All boys become monks for a time, some for only a few days, many for years, some for life.

In Thailand are the most beautiful of the Buddhist temples. In them are huge statues of the Buddha. Some are gold-covered. One resembles a great emerald. Below the large statues are smaller buddha-statues, incense burners, flowers, candles, and the offerings Buddhist worshippers have brought. Near the temples are monasteries as large as towns, surrounded by walls and guarded by statues of warrior-demons. Here monks live in small rooms. Before noon each day women bring food to the monasteries and place it on tables for the monks' meal of the day. Near the monasteries are *bots,* worship halls, where people gather to hear the monks chant scriptures and to listen as a monk reads a sermon.

Near many temples in southern Asia are trees which were grown from slips of the pipal tree under which Gautama sat the day he became enlightened and so became the Buddha.

According to the ideas of Southern Buddhists only the monks and nuns are expected to find peace and gain freedom from being born over again into a life of misery. The rest of the people can only hope that, by feeding the monks and nuns and by respecting the Buddhist religion, they themselves may, in another life, be able to be monks and nuns and get to Nirvana.

Buddhist Festivals

In Ceylon, Buddhists celebrate the most magnificent of all their festivals, the *Perahera* festival which comes in August. Sacred objects from a temple in the city of Kandy are carried through the streets in a great procession. Drummers, dancers, and elephants take part in the procession and at night flares and torches light the darkness.

Wesak, or *Kason,* which comes in May, is a most important festival among Buddhists, for it celebrates the Buddha's birth, enlightenment, and entrance into Nirvana. Devout Buddhists decorate their houses and streets for this festival and give gifts to the poor and to the monks.

Buddhism Today

In a monastery near Rangoon, Burma, a group of monks spend their lives working over ancient writings. They are Buddhist scholars studying the Three Baskets, the Buddhist scriptures. They are translating them out of the old *Pali* language in which they were originally written into languages people speak today. Buddhist missionaries study with them. From time to time ever since the Buddha sent out his followers to spread his teachings there have been Buddhist missionaries. Today Buddhists are increasingly active, telling the world what the Buddha taught.

A Buddhist university, begun in Rangoon in 1950, teaches the Buddhist way of life and the Buddhist scriptures. Near the university Buddhists have built a large assembly hall that resembles the caves in which early Buddhist monks gathered. During the years 1954-56 (the 2500th anniversary of the Buddha's birth), fifteen hundred Buddhists from many countries gathered in the "cave" for the Sixth Buddhist Council. Speakers told the gathering, "Buddhism is the religion the world needs." They said, "It is the religion that can bring peace to the world because it is a religion that teaches people to stop wanting things, to forget themselves."

There are Buddhists in many parts of the world today. Most are in Asia. A few are found in Europe. In America there are Buddhists, largely on the west coast of continental United States and in Hawaii.

Buddhism is one of the three great missionary religions active today.

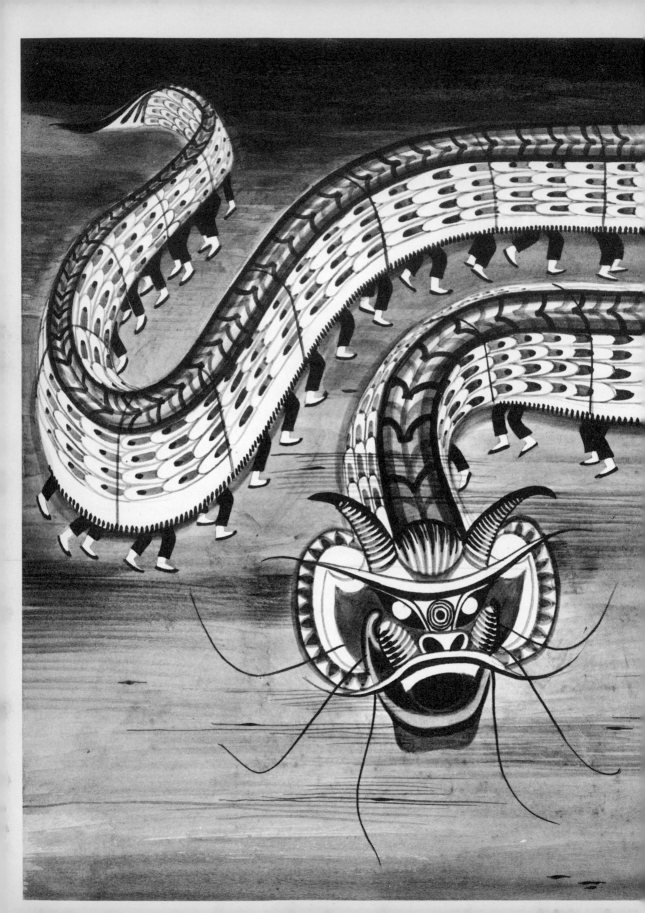

V
Chinese Religions

China, Long Ago

China is a vast land of plains, mountains, and rivers. More people live in China than in any other country of the world. One out of every four people in the world is Chinese.

Nearly four thousand years ago the Chinese built a city on the Hwang Ho (the Yellow River). They called the city Loyang and their nation the Middle Kingdom. Their nation, they thought, was the middle of the world, and the farther one went from the Middle Kingdom, the more barbaric and savage were the people.

The Chinese were a busy people interested in getting things done. Many of the products we have in the world today—chinaware, gunpowder, kites, and tea—were first used by the Chinese. The Chinese told stories about a great emperor, *Huang Ti* (the "Yellow Emperor"), who invented bricks and showed his subjects how to make articles of metal and wood. Huang Ti, they said, invented the calendar and made the first money. His wife taught women how to cultivate the silkworm and make silk cloth.

The Chinese saw that they lived in a busy universe. Those who lived by a river saw that

71

the river was always busy, all the time flowing toward the sea. It never stopped. It floated boats and broke up rocks. It made the ground fertile for growing rice. All nature, they saw, was busy. Day and night followed each other. Spring, summer, autumn, and winter came without fail. Rain fell, sun shone, rice ripened. Plants grew, sprouted blossoms, bore fruit. People were born, grew older each day, died. (Even after they died they were busy watching over the people left behind.) All the earth had a rhythm. All the universe worked together. Everything was doing something. Everything was going somewhere.

Energy and Balance

Because everything in the world was busy, the Chinese believed the world was full of energy. Sometimes it is active energy. Sometimes it is quiet energy. The active energy they called *Yang*. The quiet energy they called *Yin*. Yang is like the day, warm and bright. Yin is like the night, cool and dark. Yang is dry. Yin is moist. Yang is male. Yin is female. The Chinese made a picture to describe Yang and Yin. The picture shows a circle that resembles two tadpoles facing each other. One tadpole is always painted red or white. That is Yang, the active energy. The other tadpole is always blue or black. That is Yin, the quiet energy. If you put such a circle on a pinwheel, the breeze will whirl it around. Yang and Yin will go round and round with the breeze but will always stay opposite each other. "In the world," said the Chinese, "active energy and quiet energy are always opposite each other."

The Chinese said it was important for everyone to keep a balance of active and quiet energy in his life. This, they said, is the way of the universe. The Chinese word for "way" is *Tao* (pronounced dow). Tao, they explained, is like a road. A man who goes along a road reaches his destination. If he leaves the road he gets lost. Tao is like a river-bed. A river that flows in its bed reaches the sea. If it leaves its bed it becomes a destructive flood. Tao is like a small boat that moves smoothly down the river when people sit balanced in it. If someone gets up and moves around, the balance may be upset and the boat may turn over.

The Chinese saw that life was not always peaceful, however. There were floods and fires and earthquakes. These happened, they said, because Yang or Yin had grown too big. When Yang and Yin were exactly the same size, they balanced each other, and all went well in the world. But when one grew bigger than the other, they got out of balance and trouble occurred. People became angry and often hurt one another. Then the Chinese said, "Someone has upset the balance."

It was not always easy to determine who had upset the balance. *Shen,* or "spirits," the ancient Chinese decided. "The world is full of Shen. Many are good spirits and find ways of helping people. But some are bad and upset the happy balance of the world."

A World of Spirits

The ancient Chinese said there were spirits of the sun, moon, and planets. There were spirits in the wind, in the clouds, in hills, and streams. There was a great spirit in the skies. There was a great spirit in the earth.

It was plain to the Chinese that there were spirits everywhere and in everything. "Look at the bubbling brook," they said. "You can almost hear voices in the brook. What makes it rush so quickly downstream? Spirits, of course. These," said the ancient Chinese, "are good spirits."

Sometimes, however, brooks dried up, and there was no water for the fields. Sometimes they overflowed their banks and washed away good soil. Who can explain this? "Bad spirits," said the Chinese. "They are angry and want to cause trouble."

Ancient Chinese believed that a person became a *Kwei,* a "ghost," three years after his death. He might be a good Kwei or he might be a bad Kwei. An ancestor, then, could be a helpful ghost, or he could be a frightening ghost. Most ancestors were helpful to their families. They were, that is, if the family remembered and honoured them. Then they took care of the family and brought its members prosperity. When families forgot their ancestors, however, their ancestors neglected the families.

The honouring of ancestors, therefore, has always been important to the Chinese. As head of the family, the father kept the family together. When he died his family wrote his name on a wooden tablet and put it with other tablets to the memory of other ancestors. Each morning they honoured their ancestors by bowing before the tablets. Twice a month the head of the family told the life story of an ancestor.

The early Chinese developed a mystical symbol called the *eight trigrams (pa kua).* Their wizards used it in magical rites. Later their philosophers used it to describe the nature of life. Priests read the future in it. It had eight sides. Each side was different, yet each side corresponded to the opposite side. Ordinary people did not know exactly what it meant, but they were sure it could bring good fortune.

Emperor of Heaven

Far above all spirits and all ancestors and all good luck symbols was *Shang Ti,* "Supreme Emperor." The Chinese often spoke of *T'ien,* "Heaven," as the equivalent of Shang Ti. Heaven was over everything. Heaven, they hoped, would make all things come out right. The emperor alone could worship T'ien or Shang Ti. In Peking, the capital of China, stands the magnificent altar to Heaven. Here, twice each year, at the beginning of summer and at the beginning of winter, the Chinese emperor used to worship on behalf of the people. He asked Shang Ti to protect and prosper the Chinese Empire. It was a comfort to the Chinese people to know that Shang Ti was there, watching over them. In the meantime, they worshipped the lesser gods—gods of the field, of the family, and of the kitchen.

The Way of the Universe

One of the oldest legends in China is about Li Erh, who is known as *Lao-tzu,*[1] "the Old Philosopher." Lao, the legend says, was librarian for the emperor. No one is quite sure when he lived, but it has been guessed that he was born in 604 B.C. and lived until 524 B.C. He had learned as a child about Tao, the way of the universe. "When everyone goes along with Tao," his teachers told him, "the world is at peace and everyone is happy."

Lao observed, however, that the world was not at peace, and everyone was not happy. The Chinese Empire seemed to be crumbling. Princes disobeyed the emperor and fought among themselves. People quarrelled continuously. If Tao was the highway of the world, it seemed that a great many people were running off the highway.

Lao concluded that people evidently did not understand Tao. If they had understood, he reasoned, they would fit into the world the way pieces in a puzzle fit together. The problem, however, was to find

[1] *tzu* is the formal Chinese way of indicating honour and respect and is not a part of the name. Notice on p. 78 how it becomes a part of "Confucius."

out how the pieces fit together. But no one seemed to care about that.

Disgusted, Lao decided to leave civilization, to go west into central Asia and find peace for himself, the legends say. They add that just before he left, friends asked him to write down his ideas about Tao. He did, and the book he wrote was called *Tao Te Ching,* "The Book of the Right Way."

That is the legend. It happened so long ago that no one is quite sure how the book came to be written. At any rate, the Tao Te Ching was written by someone, probably by many wise men. It is the scriptures of the "Religion of the Right Way," *Tao Chiao,* or *Taoism.*

Not everyone understood this book. Not many people read it. In the fourth century B.C., however, a man did read it and did understand it. He was called *Chuang-tzu.* He was a scholar with a sense of humour and a love for everything in nature. It seemed to him that Tao was the religion everyone should follow.

Chuang explained the meaning of Taoism and many Chinese made Taoism their religion. Tao, Chuang reminded them, is the natural way the world goes. The river flows in its bed to the sea. The seasons never fail to follow each other, year in and year out. The birds naturally know which direction to fly each spring and autumn. No one says to the birds, "You ought to fly this way, or go in that direction." From the time they leave their nests this all comes naturally. "Everyone," said Philosopher Chuang, "ought to do things in a natural way."

"If you try to stand on tiptoe," said Chuang, "you can't stand steadily. It is not the natural way to stand. Do not try to do anything that is not natural. Do not fight against what is natural."

A swimming instructor tells his pupil not to fight the water but to float on it, to take it easy, stroke by stroke. In that way a swimmer will go farther, last longer, and be less tired. That is what Chuang was saying about everything we do.

Chuang never talked about a supreme God, because a supreme God was not necessary in his thinking. Neither were laws. Neither were human institutions. All people had to do was to live naturally, to do things naturally—that is, to live by Tao. If they did, then they would be courteous and unselfish. They would not be greedy for possessions, nor ambitious for fame.

Most people in China did not listen to Chuang any more than they had to Lao. They kept on quarrelling, struggling. Chuang said it was because they were ignorant of Tao.

Even if they were ignorant of Tao, many millions of Chinese through the centuries have called themselves Taoists, for Taoism became a religion of magic with many gods and demons, and with many priests. "If Tao is life," they explained, "then religion should be the obtaining of the essence of life for ourselves." They hoped that proper religious ceremonies could bring to worshippers long life, perhaps even life forever. The priests made charms and prepared drinks which, with the help of the gods, they said, could give babies to mothers, make crops grow for farmers, and help animals produce young. The Taoists built large, beautiful temples and filled them with pictures of gods and demons.

No one knows how many Taoists there are today. In China their temples have been closed and their monks put to work. There are probably many people in China, however, who still practise the magic of Tao. There are also Chinese Taoist temples in countries outside China.

The Way of Goodwill

The Chinese Empire was still torn by quarrels and fighting when *Mo Ti* was growing up. He lived in China in the fifth century B.C. —from 468 to 390. Since religion and the happiness of the nation always go together, Mo Ti said that the government needed to be controlled by religion.

Religion to Mo Ti was not priests and temples. It was living simply and being thrifty. "Neither individuals nor governments," said Mo Ti, "should live in luxury or spend extravagantly. Religion is treating everyone equally as brothers and sisters. It is working together with goodwill for one another."

Mo Ti said that Shang Ti, the Supreme Emperor, loves all people and wants all people to love one another. Shang Ti knows that only through goodwill can the people of the world be right, prosperous, happy, and strong.

"This is religion of common sense," Mo Ti explained. "If we do not love others we fight and quarrel and have no respect for one another. This brings trouble to everybody. To love others means to love other nations as our own, other families as our own, other persons as ourselves. When that happens there will be no more war, no more quarrelling, no more disrespect.

"If we pay attention to Shang Ti we will have love for everyone. We will want the best for everyone as Shang Ti does. But if we do not live in kindness for one another, troubles and calamities come."

For a time a few people believed that what Mo Ti taught was good. Men joined a brotherhood and promised to live simply and to follow Mo Ti's teaching.

Most people, however, preferred to love themselves better than others, their family better than other families, their nation better than other nations. So the selfishness and the quarrelling and the fighting went on and the teachings of Mo Ti were forgotten.

The Way of Right Conduct

The most famous of all Chinese teachers was *K'ung Fu-tzu*. He lived in China from 551 to 479 B.C. at the same time that Gautama the Buddha lived in India. In Europe and in America, K'ung Fu-tzu is known as Confucius.[1]

When he was a boy studying with his village teacher, he read stories about the old days of China, long before he had been born. It seemed

[1] See note on page 75.

▲   Vietnamese woman looking at hanging loops of incense in a Taoist Temple (Saigon).

to him that China must have been a happy place in those days. He read stories which said that children had obeyed their parents, people had respected rulers, and rulers had been loyal to the emperor. Everyone had behaved as he should and followed the way of peace and goodwill.

K'ung could see that the China he loved and knew had little peace and goodwill. People disobeyed the laws. The rich took advantage of the poor. The poor did not respect the rulers. "I wish," he thought, "China could be as it used to be."

When K'ung grew up he tried to teach China to be once again what it had been in the old days. He told the people how to behave. He told the governors of the different Chinese states, as well as the emperor, how they should rule. He said, "The trouble is that everyone lives without paying any attention to anyone else."

"China," said K'ung, "needs a standard by which everyone can act. If we had a standard we would have a civilization in which people would know how to treat each other, and a government that would know how to govern."

K'ung's teachings suggest five rules by which he thought people should live.

1. Rulers should rule their people wisely, and the people should be loyal to their rulers.

2. Parents should be kind to their children, and children should honour their parents.

3. Husbands should take care of their wives, and wives should obey their husbands.

4. Older children should set a good example for younger children, and younger children should respect older children.

5. Friends should be responsible for the way they behave with each other.

"If people follow the rules of human kindliness," declared philosopher K'ung, "the men of China will be true gentlemen." K'ung felt that disobedience, disrespect, selfishness, and bad behaviour are all characteristics of foolish people who have never really grown up. He said that the most perfect way to live is to remember, "What you do not want done to yourselves, do not do to others."

Master K'ung advised rulers, instructed people, and gathered around him a large number of students. He taught these students so that they might become advisers to Chinese governments. His students helped him collect and correct and copy all the stories and wise sayings of old China. These belong to five books called the *Chinese Classics*. Later, four more books were added to the Classics. These four books include the sayings and teachings of K'ung called the *Analects*.

Ever since that time Chinese people have read and studied these Classics. They have memorized parts of them. They have tried to make them the rules for good behaviour.

The most famous student of K'ung was *Meng-tzu*. In Europe and in America Meng-tzu is known as Mencius. Born in 385 or 372 B.C., he studied in the school Master K'ung had started. He memorized the Chinese Classics. Meng was disturbed because the Chinese people were ignoring the teachings of K'ung. He set out to explain these teachings to all of China. East and west, north and south, up and down the land, he went preaching, teaching, and advising rulers. When he became older and travel for him was not easy, he settled down and put into a book what he had been teaching. He wrote:

> People are good.
> Everyone naturally wants to be kind.
> Everyone naturally feels ashamed when he does wrong.
> Everyone naturally wants to be courteous.
> Everyone knows the difference between right and wrong.

"But," Meng added, "often people fight the good that is in themselves. When they do wrong it is because they are ignorant. Anyone who sticks to the goodness with which he was born, however, is truly

81

a great man, no matter how poor or unknown he may be." His book is called the *Book of Meng-tzu*, or the *Book of Mencius*.

Meng, in his book, made suggestions about the conduct of government. He said the head of a nation has the right to govern only so long as he understands and carries out the people's needs and wishes. He said, "Whatever the people understand, that is right. Whatever the people think, that is right."

K'ung had said nothing against the worship of spirits or the worship of ancestors. He thought, "Our ancestors worshipped spirits. If we behave as they did, and if we reverence our ancestors as they did, it will help us to live as they did. Life in old China was good. It was orderly. So let us keep the good order of their way of behaving."

Nevertheless, K'ung himself had paid little attention to the spirit world. "Respect the spirits," he used to say, "but stay away from them." He was more interested in making the world about him well-regulated and harmonious. He did not talk about God or about Heaven—the general word for God—for they were not important to philosopher K'ung. Heaven, for him, was just the idea of all that is good.

Meng believed as his teacher K'ung had believed. He told people: "Don't put the blame on spirits or on Heaven if things go wrong. You are responsible for the way you behave. Heaven is not responsible. Heaven does not speak," he said. "We have to look into our own minds to understand what is good and what is bad."

Nevertheless, the teachings of K'ung and of Meng became a religion called by the name of K'ung. In English we call this religion *Confucianism*.

Confucianism became a religion because:

First, it gave people rules to live by and ideals to live up to.

Second, the Chinese emperor believed that the teachings of K'ung and his pupils would help maintain good government in China. The emperor and his advisers required that anyone who wanted to

▲   Side altar in Taoist temple is laden with offerings to gods—foods and fruits in saucers and paper cups; and heaps of intricately folded paper money, coloured silver and gold, to be burned.

▶   Ceremony at Confucianist temple.

serve in the Chinese government had to study the Chinese Classics and pass an examination in them. This practice was carried on in China most of the time until the beginning of the twentieth century. China's government leaders were scholars.

Third, the government built Confucian temples. Government leaders reasoned that if people honoured K'ung as a religious leader and respected the ancient Chinese ways he praised, they would be a happy, prosperous nation.

Confucianist priests conducted worship in the temples. For many centuries great ceremonies that included the sacrifice of animals took place before the statues or wooden and stone tablets of K'ung.

Many changes came to China during the 2500 years following the time of K'ung. Occasionally, people neglected Confucianism. Occasionally, there was a revival of Confucianism. Most of the time Confucianism was the national state religion. In 1911 it ceased to be the state religion. Many in China have even ridiculed it. Yet, wherever Chinese people live, there are still those who revere and follow the teachings of K'ung.

Religious Mixture

Many Chinese became Taoists. Others became Confucianists. Whether they became Taoists or Confucianists, they kept many of the old religious ideas held in common by all Chinese since China's earliest days.

They believed in spirits, good and bad. They made offerings to gods. They honoured and made offerings to their ancestors. Now and then they went to a Confucianist temple. More often they went to a Taoist temple.

In the meantime, Buddhism came to China. The Chinese began to go to Buddhist temples as well as to Taoist temples. They asked the Taoist priests to help them have long life. They asked the Buddhist monks to conduct their funerals and to pray for them that they might go to Heaven. Taoist priests copied many Buddhist ideas. Buddhist monks copied many Taoist ideas.

In the nineteenth century new ideas came into China from Europe and America. The Chinese added to their ancient religions ideas brought by the westerners and especially by Christians.

Chinese Festivals

The Chinese have many colourful festivals reflecting this religious mixture. The *New Year* festival, in winter, is celebrated with much happiness. Temples, images, and homes are scoured clean to drive away dirt and evil spirits. On New Year's Eve doors are sealed with red paper to keep luck from leaving the house. At midnight the doors are opened to let in good luck. Sacrifices are made to the family ancestors. Outside the house a small image of a god sitting on bamboo sticks, together with a paper horse and a report on the family, is set afire. The god, in this way, takes the report of the family to Heaven.

At the time of the *Festival of the Lanterns* on the fifteenth day of the first month of the year, giant lanterns in the shape of dragons are carried lighted through the streets. These represent prayers for rain for the spring crops.

A New Order

Sun Yat Sen was a young man who eagerly studied ideas that came from the West and from Christianity. He was born in Canton, in southern China, but studied in Hawaii. He considered the Chinese Empire old-fashioned. China was weak. Her people were divided, most were uneducated and poor.

Sun Yat Sen suggested that the empire be brought to an end and that China become a democracy. The Chinese government officials wanted to put Sun Yat Sen in prison, but he escaped. For years he hid from Chinese imperial agents. When the empire fell in a revolution in 1911, Sun Yat Sen returned to help set up a democracy.

Sun Yat Sen's teachings became new principles to live by. He said that knowledge and practice—knowing about something and doing it —must go together. Some of his ideas replaced the teachings of K'ung. Sun Yat Sen taught what he called the *Three People's Principles:*

1. Chinese should love China more than anything else, even more than they love their families.

2. China should be governed by a democracy, by leaders representing the people.

3. The government should take over industry so that working people might receive better pay. Farmers, instead of working for landowners, should own their own farms.

Sun Yat Sen established an academy to train new leaders for China. These new leaders followed Sun Yat Sen's teachings. Some of them tried to continue to observe the teachings of K'ung along with those of Sun Yat Sen. Others, like *Mao Tze-tung* discarded the teachings of K'ung.

China's New Religion

Mao was one of the young men who went to Sun Yat Sen's academy. Mao was a farm boy. He worked hard. He had a bright mind and could think quickly and clearly. He could express ideas so that others understood them. Many Chinese went to Russia to study, but Mao never did. He did study the teachings of *Karl Marx,* however. In the nineteenth century Karl Marx had written a book in which he set down his thoughts about society. He called his teachings *Communist.*

Mao thought, "These teachings can help China. We don't want to be like Russia, but China can add Marx's teachings to those of Sun Yat Sen."

After Sun Yat Sen had died (in 1925), Mao began a revolution for what he called "The New Democracy." He wrote a book by that name. Just as the Book of Meng was supposed to explain and carry out the teachings of K'ung, so Mao's book was supposed to explain and carry out the teachings of Sun Yat Sen, and at the same time it explained the teachings of Karl Marx in a new way for China. Mao's followers accepted everything he said as truth. Mao believed that what he taught was what most Chinese believed and wanted. If anyone disagreed, Mao's followers talked with him until he said he understood. People soon learned it was not safe not to understand.

The number of Mao's followers increased. For a great many of them Chinese Communism became their religion. After twenty-five years Mao and his followers were powerful enough to take over the government of all China. From that time on every Chinese person was required to study the teachings of Karl Marx, Sun Yat Sen, and Mao. They met in groups for evening discussions under communist leaders. The leaders took the place of the priests and teachers of old Chinese religions. The evenings of study and discussion took the place of temple worship. Ceremonies, parades, and public confessions became a part of the new Chinese Communism.

K'ung had not thought of his teachings as a religion. But the Chinese emperor called them a religion and made Confucianism the state religion.

Mao did not think of his teachings as a religion. The Chinese government did not call them a religion. But, actually, Mao's Communism became China's new religion.

Among many Chinese, both in China and in other parts of the world, Confucianism is still looked upon as a way of life that helps to give human dignity to all people. It helps, they believe, to keep society in peace and goodwill. It inspires men and women to improve their minds. Many non-Chinese also, especially in Korea and Japan, have taught and lived by Confucian principles.

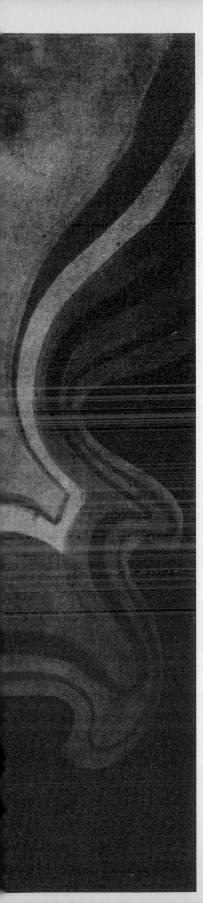

VI
Northern
Buddhism

From India to China

Ming Ti, Emperor of China, dreamed of a golden image that flew into his room as he slept. It was the image of a man sitting cross-legged in meditation. Its head glowed like the sun. Ming Ti reported his dream to his councillors. They could not interpret the dream and advised him to forget it. But one councillor said he thought the emperor had seen an image of the Buddha. Travellers across the mountains to India had been returning with tales of a religious teacher whom his followers called the Buddha, the Enlightened One.

The emperor was interested. He ordered that twelve of the wisest men in his kingdom be sent to India to bring back information about the teachings of the Buddha.

Months passed. More than a year passed. The paths over the mountains from China to India were high, wild, and dangerous. The envoys struggled along the rocky paths. Above them towered the peaks of the eastern Himalayas, covered with snow and blown by howling winds. The men shivered. Below them rushed streams of water dashing over rocks and boulders. Each man had to watch his step.

At last, one day, the twelve wise men returned. They reported to the emperor and showed him what they had brought back. They had brought statues, images of the Buddha, such as the emperor had seen in his dream. They had brought books, the teachings of the Buddha, written on leaves of the palm tree. And they had brought two yellow-robed monks to translate the teachings of the Buddha into Chinese, and to instruct the people of China in his way.

This legend is very, very old. Who can know how true it is? However it happened, it is true that in the first century A.D., when Emperor Ming Ti reigned, someone built a Buddhist monastery in China, and missionaries from India began to preach their religion to the people of China.

At first the Chinese scoffed. "This is a foreign religion," they said. "The Buddha left his family and called for monks to leave their families. How foolish! We like our families and intend to stay with them. The Buddha said life is miserable. How ridiculous! We think life is good. The Buddha said not to want possessions. How impossible! We like possessions."

Some Taoists, however, thought that Buddhism had its good points. They liked especially the Buddha's teachings about the Middle Way. The Buddha had said, "Do not go to extremes. Live a sensible, practical life." The Taoists said, "This is like the teaching of the Taoist teacher Lao. He taught that no one can live a good life if he goes to extremes in his ideas or in his habits. Everyone should live a quiet natural life."

Most of the people, however, had nothing to do with Buddhism. The Chinese admired the wisdom of the Buddhist missionaries—the Chinese admired all scholars—but they loved their homes too much to leave them to live in a monastery. The Chinese were too busy to spend their time sitting and meditating. They were too happy, and many were too rich, to want to give up all they owned. The Buddhist missionaries could not convert the Chinese.

War, Misery, and a Way Out

War came to China and split the Empire into three kingdoms. Barbarians swooped into China from Central Asia. They climbed over the Great Wall built to keep them out. They killed. They plundered. No one could stop them. For several generations this went on. Life became miserable for the Chinese. They had few opportunities to practice the orderly life of Confucianism. They looked for a way out of their trouble.

A rumour started that missionaries who knew the way out of China's misery had come over the mountains from India. They were Buddhist monks, but their teachings were not the same as those brought by the Buddhist missionaries many years before. The early Buddhists followed a strict religion, a religion for monks and nuns. The new missionaries to China said they had secret teachings that Gautama the Buddha had given to only a few. Their Buddhism was not just for monks and nuns. It was for everybody.

These Buddhists became known as *Northern Buddhists* because their teachings were popular in countries north of India. They called themselves *Mahayana Buddhists,* "Big Chariot Buddhists" because their Buddhism was big enough to give hope for everyone. (See Chapter 4.) This Big Chariot Buddhism had taken root in the rugged land of north west India. The Indian king, Kanishka, had ordered statues of the Buddha built into the hillsides—many of which can still be seen. Many Indians had begun to worship the Buddha, saying, "He deserves our respect, for he came to earth to show suffering humanity a way out of existence." New books had been written, and stories had been told about previous existences of the Buddha. These stories, called the *Jataka Tales,* are read today all around the world and many have been translated into English.

The Chinese liked the new Buddhist teachings. Confucianists especially liked the teaching that children should honour their parents. They

91

liked the rules against lying, killing, and impurity. Such teachings, they commented, would help the Chinese become good citizens. They might put an end to all the fighting that was going on. These were like the old Confucianist teachings.

But the Buddhists brought new ideas, too. They taught that people should not harm animals. Neither should they drink intoxicating liquor. Not all Chinese were ready to follow these rules. They agreed, however, that to follow the Buddhist rules would make Chinese men true gentlemen. The Chinese admired gentlemen.

The monks explained the Four Noble Truths the Buddha had taught:

1. There is suffering in the world.
2. Suffering comes from wanting things.
3. The way out of suffering is to stop wanting things.
4. The way to stop wanting things is to follow the eight-step path.

The eight-step path, the monks explained, was a way of self-control and right thought and action.

The Chinese considered the eight-step path too difficult to follow. The missionaries agreed. "But," they said, "we know a secret that the Buddha told to only his closest friends. He said there are many saviours who can help us and who will take us to their heavens when we die, if we pray to them."

This sounded attractive. The Chinese had always wanted a good and long life on earth. "But after all," they admitted, "everyone does die in the end, and then what happens?" They had no clear idea of what life was like after death. But here were the Buddhist missionaries saying it could be a very good life in a pleasant heaven if people would depend on a Buddhist saviour. Mahayana or Big Chariot Buddhists taught that there were many Buddhas ready to help.

The Chinese began to call on the Buddhists to help them with their funerals. They would ask the Buddhist monks to say "masses" and chant prayers to be sure a Buddhist saviour would take their loved one into heaven.

Buddhism grew in China and many wise men became Buddhist teachers. They translated Buddhist books from the Indian language—some of them from memory—into Chinese and wrote new books. These books are called *Shastras* and *Sutras*.

Chinese emperors who favoured Buddhism built temples for Buddhist worship and gave land and money for monasteries. Other Chinese emperors, however, persecuted the Buddhists, destroyed their temples and closed their monasteries. But the Chinese people liked the teachings of the Northern Buddhists, and gradually, Buddhism came to be practised in all parts of China, and about the tenth century reached down into Viet Nam.

From China to Korea to Japan

The Korean Peninsula reaches out from China like a long finger. Chinese rulers and Korean kings often sent messengers and exchanged goods between their countries. Educated Koreans studied Confucianism and followed many of its rules of behaviour. Soon after Buddhism became popular in China, a Buddhist monk came from North China into Korea. He interested the Koreans in this new religion and Buddhism spread quickly in the three Korean kingdoms. The Korean kings became Buddhists and ordered the building of temples and monasteries. They wanted their subjects to accept the Buddhist religion, for they hoped Buddhist practices would help them become better subjects.

In the middle of the sixth century A.D., one of the rulers, whose kingdom was on the tip of Korea, sent a golden image of the Buddha, along with sacred writings, flags, and umbrellas, to *Kimmei,* the Japanese Emperor. He explained the image in a letter.

The gifts and the golden image pleased Kimmei. The letter impressed him. The letter said: "The Buddhist religion is the religion of the great Chinese Empire and of India at the end of the earth. It has brought good fortune to my land and will to yours if you accept it."

93

Emperor Kimmei called his councillors together. He showed them the golden image and read to them the king's letter. Some of the councillors thought Japan might benefit from such a world-wide religion. Most of them, however, were afraid the *Kami,* the spirits who, according to the Shinto religion, lived in mountains and rivers, the islands and the trees, would be angry. Some of the Kami, they believed, were the ancestors of the Japanese. The councillors did not want to risk offending the Kami by bringing in a foreign religion.

The emperor's prime minister, chief of the *Soga* clan, wanted to give Buddhism a try. To him it appeared to be a more intelligent religion than that of the Kami.

The emperor and his councillors conferred together. Finally they decided, "All right, Soga, *you* take this Buddha into your house and worship it. If it brings you good luck we'll adopt Buddhism as a Japanese religion. If it brings you bad luck, we'll have nothing more to do with it."

Soga took the golden Buddha home. A short time later an epidemic broke out and thousands of Japanese became ill. Many died.

"You see," said the councillors, "our Kami are angry with us. We had better get rid of that Buddha image at once." Soga was forced to throw it into a canal, gold and all. After awhile the epidemic came to an end.

Years passed. The emperor died. When the Korean king heard that a new emperor was on the throne in Japan he decided to try again. He sent an architect to build a temple, an image-maker to fashion statues of the Buddha, two hundred sacred books to instruct the people, priests to perform Buddhist ceremonies, and a nun. He intended that the Japanese should accept the Buddhist religion.

Again the Soga clan supported the Buddhists. Again an epidemic broke out. Now the councillors were more certain than ever that the Kami were offended. This foreign religion had to go. Again the Buddha images were thrown into the canal. It appeared to be the

94

end of Buddhism in Japan. This epidemic, however, did not die out. The Japanese continued to get sick and to die. People prayed to the Kami, but still the epidemic went on. "You see," said Soga, "it is not the Kami who brought the epidemic. They are powerless to stop it. It is the Buddhas who are angry because we refuse to accept them."

Was Soga right? The councillors were not sure, but at any rate, they decided to take no more action against Buddhism.

Empress Suiki came to the throne in A.D. 588 and Buddhism began to make real progress. Her nephew, *Shotoku Taishi,* a devout Buddhist, became Regent and immediately set about making Japan a Buddhist country. Scholars had already brought Confucianist teachings to Japan from China.

Now Taishi sent scholars to China to learn all they could about both Buddhism and the Chinese form of government. Japanese priests became Buddhist monks and studied the Sutras, the Buddhist scriptures. The Japanese began to pattern their government after the government of the Chinese Empire.

Buddhism took root in Japan. Taishi built a Buddhist temple. He opened a school and staffed it with Buddhist teachers. He established a hospital, a dispensary, and a house of refuge for people in trouble. Other Japanese leaders learned from the Chinese Buddhists how to build better canals, irrigation systems, good roads, harbours, and reservoirs. In the spirit of Buddhist compassion they built houses for the poor. They planted orchards. Soon most of Japan's educated people were Buddhists.

Gradually the poorer people and the farm people of Japan became Buddhists, too. They did not wish, however, to give up the Kami of the Shinto religion. So the priests made images of the Kami and put them into the Buddhist temples. Buddhist monks decided that these Kami were really Buddhas or Buddhist saints. Now everyone was happy, for they could be Buddhists, Confucianists, and Shintoists all at the same time.

Into Tibet and Mongolia

To Tibet, in the mountains north of India, and to Mongolia, north of China, came Buddhist teachings. The Tibetans and Mongolians believed in many kinds of demons. They were afraid of these demons but, nevertheless, wanted their help. They tried to please the demons with festivals, feasting, and dancing.

The Tibetans first heard of Buddhism when, in the seventh century, their king married two Buddhist princesses, one from China and one from Nepal, the mountain kingdom between Tibet and India. The princesses begged the king to let them send for Buddhist monks. The monks came to Tibet, but the Tibetans did not understand their Buddhism. "It is too difficult," they said.

In the eighth century, however, a Buddhist missionary arrived in Tibet from Bengal on the eastern coast of India. He brought with him a new kind of Buddhism, *Tantric* Buddhism. Instead of telling people *not* to have any pleasures and *not* to want anything, this new Buddhism said, "Go ahead and indulge yourself. Satisfy your desire for food or drink or for anything. When your desires are completely satisfied you will find they have been completely destroyed. Then you will come to the place where you will not want anything and you will realize that Gautama the Buddha was right, that the only way out of trouble is not to want anything." Among Tibetan Buddhists there have been many meditating monks who have wanted nothing but to fast, endure hardships, and perform mystical practices by which they have hoped to become united with a Buddha. Tantric Buddhism teaches that everyone has a great natural store of energy within him. By practising certain sounds and movements anyone can make use of this energy to protect himself from danger. Tantric Buddhists practise magic, and worship many Buddhas and Bodhisattvas, Buddhist saints, and their female companions.

The Tibetans could understand this type of religion. It was not so

96

different from the festivals to which they were accustomed. So along with all their terrifying demons they included Buddhas. They constructed monasteries and a large number of Tibetan men became monks. The Buddhist monks of Tibet are known as *lamas*, a title which means "one who is superior." The head monks came to be considered living Buddhas, incarnations of a Buddha who has already lived on earth. When a head lama dies a search is conducted to find a child who was born at the very moment of the lama's death. If this child possesses certain secret markings and characteristics, he is considered the new living Buddha and is educated in a monastery to become a head lama. The most well-known of these living Buddhas are the *Panchen Lama,* and the Grand Lama of Lhasa, often called the *Dalai Lama.* For many centuries the lamas governed the people of Tibet until, in the middle of the twentieth century, the Chinese government took over Tibet and stripped the lamas of their political power. The Dalai Lama took refuge in India.

In the thirteenth and fourteenth centuries the Tibetan type of Buddhism became the religion of Mongolia. In the twentieth century under communism Buddhism declined. Nevertheless, many Mongolian boys still become monks and learn to sing the old Buddhist chants as they sit before great images of the Buddha.

Buddhas and Saviours

Buddhists do not worship a supreme God. The Northern or Mahayana Buddhists, however, believe there are three kinds of god-like persons.

First, they say, there are the "man buddhas," called *Manushi Buddhas.* These are persons who once lived on earth, but have reached enlightenment through meditation and have gone into Nirvana, the place of peace. There, in Nirvana, they are beyond anyone's prayers.

Second, they say, there are "enlightened beings" called *Bodhisattvas.* These are men and women who, through meditation, have arrived at

▲   Image of meditating Buddha on open lotus, Tokyo, Japan.

◄   Prayer pennants flying from the Bodnath Stupa, a famous Buddhist shrine in Nepal.

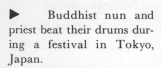   Buddhist nun and priest beat their drums during a festival in Tokyo, Japan.

Nirvana but have not yet passed into Nirvana. Because they want everyone else to enter Nirvana, also, they have postponed their own entrance in order to help others get there. They are ready to share their own merit or goodness with others and to give aid to people in any kind of distress. They are like saint-gods to whom Buddhists pray, sure of a loving response.

Third, they say, there are the "meditation buddhas," called *Dhyani Buddhas*. These Buddhas were never people of the earth. They live in the heavens and are never disturbed by what happens on earth. They are ready, however, to share their happiness and to assist anyone who prays to them.

Gautama, the founder of Buddhism, is the most famous of the Manushi or man buddhas. The Bodhisattvas, however, are more popular than the Manushi Buddhas, as well they might be, for they seem so real, so easy to understand, so easy to approach. The Bodhisattvas are pictured as kindly persons clothed in princely garments. But the simply dressed Dhyani or meditation Buddhas also became favourites with many Mahayana Buddhists. These Buddhas are pictured as monks whose faces are beautiful with peace and compassion.

A popular Bodhisattva is known to the Chinese as *Kuan-Yin* and to the Japanese as *Kwannon*. She is pictured as a gracious lady standing on a lotus flower, or on a cloud, or on a wave of the sea. On her head she sometimes wears a crown. In her arms she sometimes holds a baby. Women pray to her in the hope that she will send them children. More often she is shown with a scroll or lotus in her hands. The Japanese place images of her in temples, and on hillsides where they can be seen for miles. Hardly a home is without her image or picture. She is sometimes called "a goddess of mercy." Those who are faithful to her believe she will take them, at death, to a heaven called the "Western Paradise."

P'u-hsien, the laughing Buddha—who is really a Bodhisattva—is popular among the Chinese. His fat-bellied, laughing image is found in almost every temple courtyard, and P'u-hsien images are carried in almost every pocket, for he is supposed to bring good luck. He is said to be merciful and kind to all who pray to him.

There are many Bodhisattvas with interesting names like Samantabhadra, Manjusri, Maitreya, and Kshitigarbba. This last saint is called *Jizo* in Japan where he is a favourite of soldiers and children. His pictures sometimes show him as a fierce warrior. Sometimes they show him as a simple monk, a good friend of children. Often people pray to Jizo when a relative has died, believing he can go down to hell to carry souls up to heaven. *Maitreya,* a Buddha who has not yet come to earth, is especially well thought of by the Tibetans. He will be the next Buddha on earth, they say. And when he comes he will teach as Gautama did. In the meantime, however, they worship *Tara,* a terrifying female demon of great power.

Amida is the lord of the "Western Paradise" to which Kwannon takes her worshippers. He is a Dhyani Buddha who has never been a man on earth, but millions of Japanese and Chinese (the Chinese call him *O-mi-to*) love and worship him. Amida, they say, will take anyone to his paradise who sincerely calls out his name and asks for his help. Amida's paradise is a place of pure happiness.

Northern Buddhists say that anyone can become a buddha because Buddha is, after all, the mind that is enlightened. This enlightened mind is the realness behind everything which we think we can see or feel or describe. And this also means, Northern Buddhists explain, that anyone can become a bodhisattva, an enlightened being, who postpones his entrance into Nirvana to help others get there.

Temples

Northern Buddhists may worship and meditate at home or they may pray at one of the shrines or in one of their many temples. When they go to the temple, they leave their sandals or shoes at the temple door and enter barefoot. A Buddhist worshipper may bow his head to the ground before the image of the Buddha and repeat a prayer. He may sit on his heels or he may sit cross-legged on the floor meditating on the image of the Buddha. Before he leaves the temple he may light a stick of incense and place it in a bowl of sand, or he may fasten a printed prayer to the prayer rack. More often he will simply drop a coin in a box, rub his palms together, offer a brief prayer, and leave.

In many temples a giant image of the Buddha dominates the whole temple. Often the Buddha is shown sitting on a lotus flower, the symbol of peace. Sometimes, around his statue, are pictures and images of other Buddhas and popular Bodhisattvas. Along the temple walls are images of monks sitting cross-legged in meditation. The temple priests say these represent real monks who have become Buddhas and somewhere, deep in mountain caves, sit forever in serene meditation. Stories of Gautama's life are painted on the temple walls. These tell about his boyhood and youth, his search for wisdom, his temptations, his enlightenment, and his teachings. Sometimes the paintings show experiences which the Buddha is said to have had in earlier lifetimes.

Families and relatives go together to the temple when "masses" are said for the dead. Buddhists consider funerals important in helping the dead get to Nirvana. In the temple, incense is burned, and monks chant passages from the Sutras which the family may follow in a prayer book. The chanting often goes on for hours.

On mountaintops in Tibet and northern India stand great Buddhist monasteries and shrines from which prayer pennants wave in the wind, and near which prayer wheels turn round and round. Whenever a breeze stirs a pennant, or whenever a worshipper makes a prayer wheel turn, prayers, Buddhists believe, ascend to heaven.

In Japan there are spacious temples surrounded by gardens with many shrines and images. Some images are great and fierce, others small and delicate. In China there are hundreds of caves, brightly decorated with paintings of stories from the *Jataka Tales,* and housing Buddha statues.

Gaiety and Colour

Crowds celebrate the great festivals which are popular among Northern Buddhists. There are colourful parades and processions with gay costumes, musical instruments, much blowing of horns and shooting of firecrackers. These festivals have been popular for centuries in Tibet, China, and Japan.

Festivals and celebrations assure Northern Buddhists that Bodhisattvas will help them in this life and bring them to a good life in a pleasant heaven after death.

In May, the *Wesak* festival reminds them of the Buddha's birth, his enlightenment, and his passing into Nirvana. From Hong Kong to San Francisco, from Tokyo to New York, wherever there are Buddhists, during this festival homes, shops, and temples are decorated with flowers and bright paper lanterns.

In summer comes the *Festival of the Lanterns* when the spirits of departed ancestors are believed to return home. At the end of the festival families set afloat paper boats lighted with lanterns and supplied with food. The boats take the ancestors back to heaven or to hell. Streams, rivers, and harbours are aglow with tiny lights bobbing on the ripples.

Explaining Buddhist Teachings

Like the many bright colours of the festivals are the different sects, or denominations, of Northern Buddhism. Each has its special celebrations and festivals. Each has its favourite Bodhisattvas and Buddhas. Each tries to explain what its teachers and monks feel to be most important in Buddhism. Each has its own favourite holy book called a *Sutra*.

There are Jodo-shu Buddhists and Shin Buddhists, popular with the crowds. There are Zen Buddhists, famous for their discipline, and Tendai Buddhists who believe in study. There are Shingon Buddhists with their secret words and mysterious temple rites. These sects started in China but today are most active in Japan, so the Japanese names are given. In Japan, also, there are Nichiren Buddhists, concerned with politics and a love for Japan.

Jodo-shu and *Shin* Buddhists are called the "Pure Land Sects." They are thought to have the surest way to get to heaven. All that is necessary, they say, is to trust Amida, the Buddha of the Western Paradise, the Pure Land. There are several Pure Land "churches" in the Americas in places where Japanese have settled in large numbers.

Zen Buddhists say: "Just meditate. That is what Gautama the Buddha was doing when his mind became enlightened. Enlightenment can happen to anyone who meditates long enough. It comes like a flash of light. But you must concentrate and not let your mind wander." Zen Buddhist monks practise sitting still for hours, controlling their muscles, their breath, and their thoughts.

Zen Buddhism was popular among the warriors of old Japan, for it provided them with a way of self-discipline. Zen Buddhists developed the art of flower arranging and the making of simple, beautiful paintings and poems. They gave the Japanese their famous tea ceremony.

The *Tendai* sect has many scholars and many followers in Japan. It began in China with a monk, *Chih K'ai,* who said Buddhism was so difficult that the Buddha must have taught different ideas for different people. It depended on how much they could understand. Chih K'ai advised the monks in his monastery, "Learn all you can from your Buddhist teachers. Read all the Buddhist books you can and take part in Buddhist ceremonies. They are all helpful."

Shingon, or the "True Word," sect is preferred by many uneducated people. They are attracted by the magic words and chants, the mysterious ceremonies conducted by the priests, and like the music and the firecrackers that are part of these ceremonies. Such ceremonies, they are sure, can control the weather, bring good health and good luck, cure sickness, and rescue the dead from hell. Shingon Buddhists admire the many Buddhas and Bodhisattvas who, in their minds, are gods and goddesses. Shingon priests teach that even those who do not understand all of Buddhism can live a good life by loving the Buddhist temples and Buddhist worship. Many Japanese boys and girls study in schools run by this sect.

Nichiren Buddhism started in Japan in the thirteenth century. A Buddhist monk was sitting on a mountainside early one morning, reading a Sutra and meditating. He looked at the rising sun and felt inspired. "The Buddha is in the sun," he thought. "And the truth of the Buddha is in this book I am reading." In the Sutra he read that one day a Bodhisattva would come to earth to teach people true Buddhism. "I am that Bodhisattva," the monk decided. "I will teach true Buddhism to the people of Japan." He called himself Nichiren.

Nichiren preached against corruption in the Japanese government, and commanded the Japanese to love Japan loyally enough to clean up its politics. "If you do not," he warned, "Japan will be conquered by a foreign people."

About that time a great navy of Mongolians attacked Japan. The Mongolians were driven away, but many Japanese were sure that this was the judgment Nichiren had predicted.

Great numbers of Japanese began to follow Nichiren. He taught from the Sutra that had inspired him on the mountainside. He preached patriotism. He required his followers to take three vows: "I will be the pillar of Japan; I will be a great ship for Japan; I will be eyes to Japan."

In the middle of the twentieth century a branch of this sect, the *Soka Gakkai,* grew rapidly. Millions of Japanese joined it. Parades, political rallies, and loyalty to Japan are part of their Buddhism.

Northern Buddhism Today

In China there are still Mahayana or Northern Buddhists who honour the Buddha although, under China's communist government, many Chinese gave up Buddhism.

In Japan, millions of Japanese worship at Buddhist temples or are associated with one of the many Buddhist sects. Some of the sects are growing with a new popularity. They are printing new books on Buddhism and conducting kindergartens and schools for their children. The monks of the temples take care of funerals for many Japanese.

In Korea there are still temples and monasteries, but most Koreans are no longer active Buddhists.

In the Philippine Islands, in Malaysia and Singapore, in Indonesia, in Thailand, in Burma, in the West Indies, in the United States of America, and wherever the Chinese have gone to live there are temples and monasteries for Chinese Buddhists.

Japanese Buddhists in some cities (especially in Hawaii and on the American west coast) have founded "churches" patterned after Protestant Christian churches. They have Sunday services with hymn singing and sermons, Sunday school classes, and youth groups.

Northern Buddhists are translating books of Buddhist poetry and meditations into other languages and many people in the world, Buddhist or not, are finding in them beauty, wisdom, and inspiration.

▶ Buddha images in a temple, Kyoto, Japan.

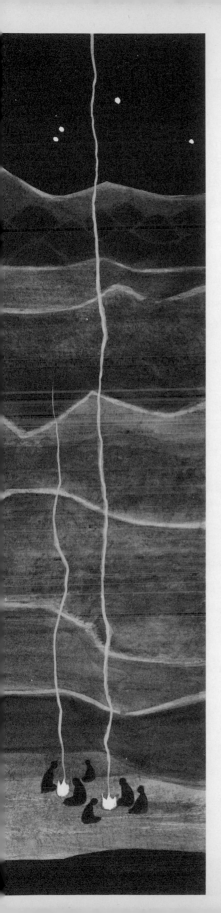

VII
Judaism

Tribes of the Desert

The Tigris and Euphrates rivers flow from the mountains of western Asia southeast to the Persian Gulf.

The Nile River flows north from Central Africa through lakes and plains and desert to the Mediterranean Sea.

Along these rivers, four thousand years ago, were rich cities, fertile fields, and great temples.

Between the great civilization along the Nile and the great civilization along the Tigris and Euphrates there lay a vast desert area. There was no connection between the two except along a narrow strip of land on the eastern end of the Mediterranean. This strip of land was fertile and to desert tribes looked very pleasant.

Along the fringes of all these lands and in the desert, nomadic tribes wandered. They moved from oasis to oasis and to the short-lived desert streams. They went wherever there was pasturage for their animals and the chance of food for themselves. They still do. Sometimes they have been forced to move into the fertile land near the Mediterranean or to the cities of the Nile, of the Tigris and Euphrates to beg for food. Then they have returned to the desert. But always some tribes remained to work for the people of the land, to settle among them, even, sometimes, to conquer them.

Their religion, however, has borne the marks of the desert from which they came. There in the desert no one could explain where the precious water came from. It appeared in springs and wells and in occasional brooks and streams. No one could explain, either, where groves of trees sprang from, why sandstorms blew, or what made snakes sly and wild animals cunning. "It must be the *els* that are in them," the desert tribes thought. Els were powerful spirits, superhuman beings, or even gods. At night, surrounded by a wide desert, covered by the wide starry sky, it was easy to feel the presence of the els, even of some great God above all the els.

Chosen by God

From these desert tribes came the people called *Hebrews* who conquered and settled the land on the eastern end of the Mediterranean Sea, called Canaan. They had a strong sense of being led by God. God, they said, had created the world and man for a purpose. He had chosen them, the Hebrew people, to carry out his purpose. The Hebrews told stories about their ancestors and their history and how God had always been with them, leading and directing them.

They told about *Abraham* whom they called the father of the Hebrews. Abraham was a chieftain in a tribe that had wandered for centuries along the northern borders of the desert, they recounted. This tribe had settled for a time close to the ancient city of Ur near the Euphrates River. There, in the land that worshiped the moon-god, *Sin,* Abraham had been born. From there his tribe moved northward along the edge of the desert until it found pasturage near a place called Haran.

Under the stars at night, the Hebrews said, Abraham thought about God. He even heard God speak to him. Abraham felt that God had chosen him, Abraham, for his own. He believed that this God who had chosen him was more powerful than the spirits that lived in rocks and trees and sacred groves and were worshipped by the desert tribes. He was more powerful than the demons in snakes and wild animals and sandstorms. He was more powerful than the wooden household gods his people carried with them. He was more powerful than the moon-god, Sin, whom the people of Ur worshipped. Abraham reached out beyond all gods and all spirits to worship this powerful God.

God, the Hebrews said, directed Abraham to leave the land of his birth and go to a new land. He would go with the tribe and protect them. He would show them where to settle down. He would make them a great nation. So the tribe folded its tents and drove its flocks south-westwards to Canaan. In Canaan Abraham's son Isaac was born and his grandson Jacob. There Abraham learned many things about his God. He learned that his God did not want the sacrifice of human beings. Abraham's neighbours often killed a son or daughter on an altar as a sacrifice to their gods. Abraham discovered that his God did not want the death of any human being.

The Hebrews told about Abraham's descendants moving from Canaan when food became scarce and settling on the rich lands of the Nile delta. Egypt, at that time, was ruled by the *Hyksos*, "Shepherd kings," who were themselves foreign conquerors. They were friendly to these strangers from Canaan and let them settle in Goshen, a fertile tract of land on the north-east border of Egypt. Here they raised sheep, goats, and cattle. At least one of them, Joseph, became a high government official. All this happened sometime between the years 1900 and 1600 B.C.

Leader of His People

The most famous story in all the history of the Hebrews, however, begins with the rescue of a baby boy. The Egyptians had driven out the Shepherd Kings and a new line of Egyptian kings, or *pharaohs*, came to the throne. One of them initiated a great building programme. He planned new temples for Egyptian gods, new canals for irrigation, new cities for storing grains. He needed cheap labour to develop his projects. Where could he get it? He thought of the foreigners who lived in Goshen. Who were these people, anyway? They weren't Egyptians. Why were they living on some of Egypt's best land? Their population was increasing rapidly! Suppose, thought the Pharaoh, a hostile army invaded Egypt and these people sided with the enemy! Better do something about them! The Pharaoh, the Hebrews said, ordered the adults of the tribe drafted into the labour corps and put to work as slaves on the building projects. He ordered the killing of all baby boys born to them.

The Hebrews told about one baby boy who was rescued by the Pharaoh's daughter. She gave him the name *Moses*.

Moses grew up in the palace, but he always knew he was not an Egyptian. One day, when he saw an Egyptian overseer beating a slave of his people, Moses, in anger, struck the Egyptian and killed him. Moses fled, in fear, to Midian in north-west Arabia. He became a shepherd and herded the sheep of a chieftain-priest. He married the priest's daughter.

Here Moses felt safe. Even so, he was not happy. He thought about his own people, slaves in Egypt. He heard there was a new pharaoh on the throne who was oppressing them more than ever. He longed to free them. But what could he, a poor shepherd, do?

One day, the Hebrews recorded, as Moses led the sheep to the slopes of a barren mountain in the western desert, Mt. Sinai, he saw a bush aflame with fire. He heard a voice saying to him: "Moses, Moses, I am the God of your father, the God of Abraham, the God of Isaac, the God of Jacob." Moses was frightened. Here was a God who was more than the els that lived in bushes and stones. Here was the God his forefathers had believed in, a strong, forceful God. The voice continued, "I know the suffering of my people in Egypt. Go back to Egypt and free them." He revealed to Moses his name. The voice said, "I am who I am, the one who always is—*Yahweh*."

Moses was afraid to go back to Egypt. He thought up excuses. Who would listen to him? He was a man with a price on his head. How could he go to the Pharaoh? How could he convince the Pharaoh to let his people go, or even convince his people to follow him?

Nevertheless, Moses went back to Egypt. He asked the help of his brother Aaron and together they went to the Pharaoh to demand the freedom of their people. The Pharaoh refused. Moses and Aaron organized the people and in the dark of night led their escape from Egypt. The Pharaoh sent soldiers, equipped with fast chariots, to pursue them, but they eluded the Egyptians and fled across an arm of the Red Sea (sometimes called the Reed Sea) into the desert. They moved on through the barren land and camped near Mt. Sinai.

Once again the descendants of Abraham were wanderers in the desert. Sometimes they complained and wished they were back in Egypt. But all the time they were learning to live together as one nation. Moses often climbed Mt. Sinai, the mountain where he had first heard the voice of Yahweh. There in the quiet of the mountaintop he became sure of Yahweh's plan.

For centuries the descendants of Abraham told stories of the difficult days when Moses and the tribes of Abraham wandered in the desert. They told stories about the time Moses came down from the mountain carrying two large tablets of stone on which were written God's words to the Hebrew people as to who he was and what he expected of his people. The tablets said: "I am the Lord your God who brought you out of the land of Egypt, out of the state of slavery. Because of this, therefore,

1. You must not make any other gods your God.

2. You must not make any image of anything in the world and worship it.

3. You must not speak the name of God lightly.

4. Remember to keep the seventh day of the week sacred to God. You have six days for doing all your work.

5. Honour your father and your mother.

6. You must not commit murder.

7. You must not commit adultery.

8. You must not steal.

9. You must not bring false charges against your neighbour.

10. You must not set your heart on having what belongs to someone else.

The Hebrews called these rules the *Ten Commandments*. The first four commandments told the people how to worship God. The last six were rules for living together. The people put the tablets with the commandments into a box known as the *ark*. The ark, they carried with them wherever they went. To them it represented God's presence.

Abraham's descendants had grown in their sense of being God's people. Their religious leaders later wrote that, out there in the desert, Yahweh made a covenant, an agreement, with them. They would be Yahweh's chosen people. He would guide them and protect them. But they, in turn, had to *obey* Yahweh's commandments. If they did not, Yahweh would punish them.

Canaan Again

Moses died and his place was taken by Joshua, a leader who had been close to Moses. Joshua knew the tribes would meet opposition in trying to enter Canaan. But he was sure God wanted them to return to this land. This was the land Yahweh had promised Abraham's descendants! They were Abraham's descendants! Joshua organized a military expedition and led them across the Jordan River to conquer central Canaan. They came to be known as Hebrews, "boundary-crossers." For years the Hebrew tribes fought with local Canaanite tribes and with those who lived in many small cities. Gradually the Hebrews grew in power and in control of the land.

The Hebrews were no longer people on the move. They were no longer shepherds going from place to place looking for pasturage for their sheep. They were now a settled people trying to farm the land, but they had never been farmers raising crops before. They had much to learn and looked to their farmer neighbours, the Canaanites, for help. The Hebrews saw that the Canaanites worshipped baals, farm-gods. *Baal* meant "owner," and the Canaanites said it was the baals who owned the land and were responsible for its fertility. The Hebrews saw that the Canaanites made shrines to the baals and set them on their farms, or where springs burst from the earth, or on hilltops. Some of the shrines, they saw, contained images of bulls and snakes, symbols of the baal's power to make the land fertile. They watched as the Canaanites sacrificed animals, fruit, and grain to the baals to per-suade them to give good crops. The Hebrew farmers began to wor-ship the baals, too. Those whose conscience troubled them because they were worshipping the baals decided, "When we worship the baals we are really worshipping Yahweh."

Men Who Spoke for God

In time, the Hebrew tribes united under the rule of kings. The great king *David* (about 1000 B.C.) made Jerusalem his capital city and set up a *tabernacle,* a "tent," for the ark that held the Ten Command-ments. David's son, Solomon, built a temple in *Jerusalem,* and Jeru-salem became an important centre for Hebrew worship.

After Solomon's death, the new nation broke into two kingdoms, each with its own capital. The southern kingdom, Judah, with its capital at Jerusalem, kept that city as the centre of its worship. The northern kingdom, Israel, established its capital in the city of Shechem and later in Samaria, which became the centre of its worship. There remained in both kingdoms many small shrines for the worship of Yah-weh, and others for the worship of the baals. Some of the kings of these two kingdoms were able men who remembered the covenant the Hebrews had made to obey Yahweh, but others neglected the religion of their fathers. One of these, King Jeroboam, made two golden bull images for the people to worship. "These are the gods who brought our ancestors out of Egypt," he told them.

Another king, Ahab, married a baal-worshipping princess from Tyre, a city to the north. She brought with her baal-priests and made them priests in Yahweh's temple. *Elijah*, the story says, was a prophet, a man who spoke for Yahweh, who called the baal priests together and challenged them to prove that their god was real. "Ask your god to send down fire to light a sacrifice," he commanded. The priests of baal made an altar and prepared a sacrifice. All morning they called on their god, but nothing happened. Then Elijah prepared a sacrifice and prayed to Yahweh, and fire came down like a bolt of lightning and burned his sacrifice. "Yahweh, he is God," cried the frightened people.

There were other men who spoke for God. Israel, the northern kingdom, grew rich and prosperous. At least it was rich and prosperous for the aristocracy, the upper classes. But while the rich were growing richer, the poor found it harder to make a living. *Amos,* a shepherd and gardener, often brought his produce from a village in Judah to the busy markets of Israel. He observed the fine houses of the rich and the hovels of the poor. He saw women concerned only about their make-up, their jewels, and their clothes, and men drinking themselves into unconsciousness. He watched the people who were outwardly religious, celebrating festivals at the shrines, but not really worshipping God.

Amos was indignant. He believed that a nation which had broken its covenant with Yahweh would destroy itself. He went to Bethel, the royal shrine of Israel, and began to speak his mind. He told the worshippers there that a righteous and just God demands righteousness and justice among his people. The priest was annoyed. "If you have any preaching to do, go back to Judah to do it!" he said. "Don't you know that this is the royal shrine, the king's temple?"

Amos carried on preaching. "I am a messenger sent from God to tell the king and the people that Israel will be conquered and the population carried off to another land unless you change your ways. Hate evil, love what is good," he said, "be just in all your dealings, then God will be with you." But the people did not listen, and eventually Israel was conquered and many of its people carried away from their homeland.

There was another man in the northern kingdom of Israel who spoke for God, also, but in a different way. His name was *Hosea.*

Hosea said he had a wife whom he loved very much, but his wife did not love him and left him for other men. Hosea set out to look for her. He searched until he found her. He brought her home again and loved her as he always had. Hosea thought, "If I, a man, can love my wife who ran away from me, how much more can God love Israel whose people have turned away from him and are worshipping other gods."

Hosea felt that God loved his people with a love that never came to an end. But, like Amos, he was sure they would be destroyed if they did not stop lying, stealing, swearing, and burning incense to idols.

In the kingdom of Judah, a country preacher, *Micah,* told the people, "You will be destroyed because you have lost your faith in God. You are trying to win God's favour by sacrificing your animals, your fruits and grain, and even your children. But that is not what God wants. He wants you to show kindness to each other, to be just in all your dealings, to be humble when you worship God." To Micah, justice, kindness, and faithfulness to God represented true religion.

In the capital city of Jerusalem a man, named *Isaiah,* from an important family, perhaps a branch of the royal family, spoke to the king himself. He knew Judah was in danger but he advised the king not to make alliances with foreign countries in the hope of saving Judah. He saw God as the moving force behind all history and told the king to put his faith and confidence in God. "Only when you rely on God will you be strong," he said.

115

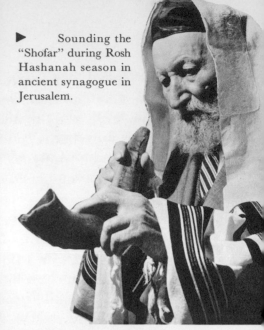

Sounding the "Shofar" during Rosh Hashanah season in ancient synagogue in Jerusalem.

◄ Young man holds a scroll of the Torah. Velvet cover has two Lions of Judah and tablets representing Ten Commandments.

▼ Young student in Israel, head covered with traditional skullcap, washes his hands symbolically at morning prayers.

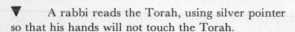

▼ A rabbi reads the Torah, using silver pointer so that his hands will not touch the Torah.

Isaiah looked forward to a day when the Hebrews would have a new kind of king, a king who would rule with love. Isaiah called him the Prince of Peace, the *Messiah,* which means the "one anointed." When that king rules, Isaiah said, Jerusalem will lead in bringing peace to all nations. As Micah did, Isaiah too, looked forward to a day when all nations would turn to Jerusalem and worship the God of the Hebrews.

Amos, Hosea, Micah, and Isaiah spoke to the Hebrews in the eighth century B.C.

In most religions, the people's early belief in spirits or nature gods, and their ceremonies to make the land fertile and productive, remained part of their religion. Not so with the Hebrews. Hebrew religious leaders continually fought against this tendency and insisted on the worship of the one, invisible Yahweh who was a God of justice and righteousness.

In 621 B.C., in the reign of the young king *Josiah,* the priest reported to the king that workmen, repairing the temple, had found a law book. When the king read it he realized how far away the people were from keeping Yahweh's laws. He ordered the shrines and sanctuaries throughout the country to be demolished. Hereafter, everyone was to worship at the Temple in Jerusalem. In this way King Josiah hoped that he could unite the people in loyalty to one religion and one God. He commanded the people to keep all the laws written in this law book.

The book is known as *Deuteronomy* which means "second law," for it repeats many of the laws found in other books of the Hebrews. It demands justice for all, good treatment of slaves, thoughtfulness for the poor, and the worship of Yahweh alone. The most important part of the book is the *Shema.* Shema means "hear," the first word of the instruction that says: "Hear, O Israel, Yahweh is our God, Yahweh alone. You shall love Yahweh with all your heart, and with all your soul, and with all your strength. These words which I am giving you this day you shall keep in your heart; and you shall teach them diligently to your children, and shall talk about them when you sit in your house and when you go on a journey and when you lie down and when you get up." The Shema became, and still is for Jews everywhere, the heart of their religion.

Refugees

The prophets had spoken for God, but people carried on living as they always had. Israel was destroyed in 722 B.C. by the armies of Assyria, the mighty power to the north east. Israel's people were deported to many parts of the Assyrian Empire. The people of Judah thought that as long as the temple stood in Jerusalem they would be safe. *Jeremiah,* a young man from a family of priests, had other ideas. He told the people: "You talk about the 'temple of the Lord, the temple of the Lord' as though it can protect you. It is not going to the temple that can protect you. God demands faithfulness to him and fair treatment of all people." Jeremiah saw the approach of armies from the east, from Babylon, an empire based in the Tigris and Euphrates river country. He predicted the fall of Jerusalem to the Babylonians. Yet, he believed Yahweh would not desert his people. After they had been punished, he would make a new covenant with them. This time, however, the covenant would not be between Yahweh and the nation. It would be between Yahweh and the individuals of the nation. Jeremiah declared that individuals as well as nations are responsible to God. A nation behaves as the individuals in the nation behave.

In 586 B.C. the Babylonian armies captured Jerusalem and deported most of the people to Babylon. The Hebrews were refugees in a foreign land, but the prophets still spoke. *Ezekiel* was a prophet who dreamed of the time when the people would be permitted to return to their homeland and would rebuild Yahweh's temple. He called himself "watchman to the household of Israel" and kept alive the hope of returning home.

One of the greatest of all the prophets appeared at this time. His name is not known. His message is found in the *Book of Isaiah*. Sometimes he is called Second Isaiah. The refugees were asking: "Why do we have to suffer like this? The Babylonians are worse than we and they are not suffering!" This prophet answered: "Your suffering is part of God's plan to save the whole world. Babylon, like other conquering nations, will fall, and you will go back home. After that happens the world will see the glory of God."

The Hebrews had once thought of Yahweh as the God of the Hebrews only. Other people had other gods, but Yahweh was their God and they were Yahweh's people. The unknown prophet insisted: "Yahweh is the only God. There is no other." He told the Hebrews that God had chosen them to carry his message to the world. They were to be God's suffering servant in order to save the world for his purpose. Later on, many Jews who read the message of this unknown prophet, saw in his words a promise of the Messiah whom they were eagerly expecting.

Far from their homeland, the Hebrew way of life changed. Those who had come from Judah became known as *Jews*. They could no longer go to the temple in Jerusalem to worship. Many forgot Yahweh and followed Babylonian gods. Others said, "How can we remember the laws of Yahweh? How can we keep our children from following the Babylonian gods?"

In an effort to preserve their religion they met together in each other's homes. They talked about the prophets and read the Law. There were men among them who were learned in the Law and explained it to the people. By and by the Jews began to meet together every *sabbath*, the seventh day of the week. They called the place where they met the *synagogue*. Synagogue is a Greek word meaning "assembly." The synagogue became, and still is, a place where Jews assembled for instruction and worship.

Home Again

In 538 B.C., *Persia* conquered Babylonia, and *Cyrus,* the Persian king, said the Jews could go home if they wanted to. Many did. They rebuilt the walls of Jerusalem, rebuilt the temple under the leadership of *Ezra,* who believed firmly in the Law. They continued the practice, begun in captivity, of meeting together every sabbath, and they set about to make Judaism a strong religion. Marriage with non-Jews was forbidden. Worship on the sabbath day was strictly enforced. Worship in the temple became important again, and the priests grew powerful. The Jews went to the temple for religious ceremonies and to present their offerings of grain and animals to Yahweh, but they went to the synagogues to learn the *Torah,* the law codes, of their scriptures. Teachers, later called *rabbis,* taught in the synagogues. *Scribes,* or writers, copied and explained the Torah, and religious men wrote new books about God and his relations with the Jews.

Anchoring the Faith

Festivals became important in anchoring the lives of the Jews to their religious faith. These festivals, with some changes in their meaning and in ways of celebrating them, continue to this day as part of the religious observance of Jews everywhere.

The *Passover* festival—*Pesach* or the "Feast of Unleavened Bread"—was a spring festival of thanksgiving for the new lambs and sprouting grain. It came to be associated with the escape of the Hebrews from Egypt. In the early days of the festival a lamb was eaten on the first night of the celebration. Today, this has been replaced by the *Seder* feast on the first night of Passover. It is a time when all the family gathers together. In eating specially prepared foods that are symbolic of the trials of the Hebrews in Egypt, and in hearing again the story of their escape, Jews everywhere are challenged anew to seek freedom from any kind of bondage.

Seven weeks later, at the beginning of summer, comes *Pentecost—Shabuoth* or the "Feast of Weeks." Originally each family brought the first fruits of the barley harvest to the temple as a thanks offering to God. Gradually this festival came to include not only thanks for the harvest but also for the giving of the Law on Mt. Sinai.

The "Feast of Trumpets," later called *Rosh Hashanah,* or "New Year," was celebrated in the autumn. At the beginning of the new year a ram's horn called Jews to penitence. Rosh Hashanah has sometimes been called the Day of Judgment, for on that day all the people of the earth are said to pass before God and to be given a mark in the book of life or the book of death.

The ten days following Rosh Hashanah are the days of repentance ending with *Yom Kippur,* the solemn "Day of Atonement." It was on the Day of Atonement that the priest urged the people to repent of their sins and to turn from doing wrong to doing God's will. As he confessed his own sins and the sins of Israel, the priest placed his hands on a live goat. This *scapegoat,* as he was called, was then driven off into the wilderness carrying the sins of the people with it. During this service, when the priest uttered the name Yahweh all the people fell on their faces. The old ceremony is gone but the day still remains a solemn one and many Jews, who may not go to the synagogue at any other time of the year, go on the Day of Atonement. Rosh Hashanah and Yom Kippur are called high holy days.

At *Sukkoth,* the "Feast of Booths," which comes in the autumn, the Hebrews gave thanks to God for the plentiful fruit harvest. Later they decorated their synagogues with fruits and flowers. They built booths of vines and leaves and lived in them during the eight days of the festival to remind themselves of God's goodness to their ancestors who lived in crude shelters in the desert. Today, a booth in the synagogue has, for many Jews, taken the place of the booths they used to build at home. For other Jews, however, building a booth and eating their meals in it remains an important part of the Sukkoth celebration.

The Persians ruled the Jews for about two hundred years. Then the Greek-speaking emperors of the Egyptian and Syrian empires ruled them for about another 160 years. The Jews did not rebel so long as no one tampered with their religion. One king of *Syria, Antiochus Epiphanes,* however, wanted to unite his empire in worship of the Greek gods, *Zeus* and *Dionysus.* He set up shrines to Zeus throughout his empire. In the temple in Jerusalem he not only built an altar but sacrificed a pig to Zeus. This angered the Jews. To them the temple was sacred to Yahweh. No other god was to be worshipped in it. Nothing unclean or unfit as a pig was to be brought into it.

Under the leadership of an old priest and his five sons, called the *Hasmoneans,* the Jews revolted in 168 B.C. and eventually drove out the Syrians.

The victory of *Judas Maccabeus* over the Syrians and the rededication of the temple is celebrated today in *Hanukka,* the "Feast of Lights," which means "dedication." Hanukka falls in late November or early December. For eight days, in homes and synagogues, one candle is lighted each night until eight are burning brightly in commemoration of the rekindling of the temple lamps.

In the second century and for several generations after, many books were written to encourage the Jews to be true to their faith in spite of their troubles. These books used word pictures and stories which only Jews could understand. Scholars call these writings *apocalyptic* which means "uncovering what was secret." They promised that God's Messiah would soon come. The most famous of these books is called the book of *Daniel.*

For about eighty years (142-63 B.C.) the Jews were an independent people. But in 63 B.C. the Romans occupied their country. Many Jews were certain the nation had endured all it could. Surely the long awaited Messiah would come. A century later a few were certain the Messiah had come in the person of Jesus of Nazareth. But most of the Jews still looked for the Messiah's coming. At last some of the Jews could not wait any longer and rebelled in A.D. 66. In retaliation in A.D. 70 a Roman army destroyed the Jewish Temple. It was never rebuilt. In A.D. 135, after another bloody revolt, the Romans crushed the Jews and barred them from putting a foot inside Jerusalem.

Through their many captivities Jews had scattered into many countries. Now they were more widely scattered than ever. Throughout the Roman Empire into Europe, North Africa, and south west Asia they went. Some went east in Asia beyond the Roman Empire. Through the centuries they have gone to every part of the world. Yet, wherever they have gone they have formed Jewish communities, met in synagogues, and kept their Jewishness.

Even without a homeland they have been able to maintain their religion. Not until 1948 when the new Jewish nation of Israel was created, did they again have a homeland.

The Hebrew Bible

Through the years the Hebrews wrote down the things they learned about Yahweh. They put into books the laws of Yahweh, the history of their people as they followed or forgot Yahweh, and the messages of the prophets. They gathered together the Psalms, the songs of praise their poets had written, and the proverbs and other teachings of their wise men.

In A.D. 69, shortly before Jerusalem was destroyed by the Romans, a rabbi, *Johanan ben Zakkai*, escaped from the city and fled to Jamnia (sometimes called Jabneh), a town near the shores of the Mediterranean Sea. There he started a school to study the Torah, the written laws of the Jews. Although the Torah and the books of the prophets were already considered Jewish scriptures, Jewish scholars at Jamnia decided toward the end of the first century which of their religious writings should be used to make up the Hebrew Bible.

The Torah, the first five books of the Bible, is for Jews the most important part of their scriptures. The Torah contains all the laws

123

that through the centuries have helped the Jews live as Yahweh's people.

Other Religious Books

As times changed, however, the Jews needed help in knowing what some of the laws meant. The rabbis interpreted the laws for them. If the law, for example, said, "wash your hands before you eat," the rabbis, in order to show what it meant really to wash one's hands, specified just how far up the wrist a person must wash. They defined just what any Jew could do and should not do in keeping the sabbath day "holy," set apart for Yahweh. They gave explanations of their scriptures to guide and direct the lives of the Jews. These comments were memorized but not written down. A leading scholar at Jamnia, *Rabbi Akiba,* classified them, but it was not until about A.D. 220 in Galilee that they were at last written down. Under a rabbi, who is sometimes called *Judah the Patriarch,* the comments and legal decisions of rabbis for six centuries were collected into a vast work called the *Mishnah,* "Recited Law." The Mishnah became for Jews almost as important as the Torah itself.

The rabbis then began to interpret the Mishnah. At the same time they continued to search out and record every bit of Jewish learning they could find. Jewish scholars in Babylonia put this material together in a book known as the *Gemara,* meaning "completion."

All these interpretations of rabbis through the centuries were collected into a book of sixty-three sections, called the *Talmud* which meant "study." The Talmud gives directions for every detail of a Jew's life. Like a fence, it surrounds the Law with interpretations.

The Jews were scattered all over the world and were often the victims of bloody persecutions. They were made to live apart from other people in sections of cities called *ghettos.* Yet, through the centuries, the Mishnah and the Talmud have helped Jews remain Jews no matter where they have lived or what persecutions and difficulties they have had to endure.

In ancient times the prayers of the Jews were brief and were recited only on special occasions. They were always memorized and never written down. After the temple was destroyed the rabbis continued to create prayers, poetry, and hymns, and about A.D. 500 the prohibition against writing them down was dropped. In time two types of prayer books came into use. The *Siddur,* meaning "arrangement," had weekday and sabbath prayers. The *Mahzor,* meaning "repetition," contained prayers, poetry, rules, scripture readings for the holidays, and explanations of the material in the book. These collections differed in different countries. After printing was invented, a few of them became more widely used than others. Today, each branch of Judaism has its own revised prayer book.

In the twelfth century, a Spanish Jew named *Moses Maimonides* condensed the traditional laws and made them more understandable and easier to study. He also summarized the Jewish faith into thirteen principles. These principles reminded Jews that God was the only God and that his Law came from heaven and could not be changed. Maimonides said that by using their minds men could come to a better understanding of God.

Judaism Today

In the twentieth century, Jews who called themselves *Zionists* actively urged all Jews to return to the land of their forefathers. They declared this would fulfill God's promise to their ancestors and give Jews safety from persecution. Their organization brought many persecuted Jews back to the land from which their forefathers had gone as refugees. In 1947, the United Nations Assembly voted to create the new nation of Israel as a homeland for the Jews. In 1948 Israel became a nation. Many oppressed Jews from Europe went to live in Israel. Hebrew is the national language of Israel. In building a new Israel, the government leaders frequently refer to the historical records in the Hebrew scriptures. As a nation they observe the old Jewish festivals. Judaism, however, is not a state religion. There is no centre for Jewish worship in Jerusalem as there was in the days of the early Hebrews.

The majority of Jews live in other nations around the world. Judaism has several branches.

One branch is called *Orthodox Judaism.* Orthodox Jews say that the Jews are still God's chosen people. They believe that someday a Messiah will come and set up his kingdom in Jerusalem. They believe that God's perfect revelation of himself is found in the Law. They hold to Maimonides' set of thirteen principles and follow the teachings of the Talmud. They are careful to keep the sabbath day as a special day, sacred to God, to prepare their food according to Jewish dietary rules, and to keep all the Jewish festivals. Rosh Hashanah and Yom Kippur are especially important. In their synagogues women sit in a separate place, usually a balcony or gallery, apart from the men. Only boys and men become members of the synagogue. There are many orthodox Jews in America, but the majority live in Israel.

Another branch is called *Reform Judaism.* Reform Jews are found mostly in the United States. They believe God revealed himself in the Law but has gone on revealing himself in many ways. They do not look for a Messiah. They believe in God as the only God and believe people should live good and upright lives. They observe the Jewish festivals and holidays, although not always in the traditional way. They adapt their ways to the country in which they live. They have done away with a separate gallery for women and introduced the family pew where the family sits together. Girls as well as boys become members of the synagogue. Women have equality with men in the life of their synagogues. Reform Jews often hold services on Sunday instead of on Saturday, the Jewish sabbath. In their synagogue services they use both Hebrew and the language of the country.

A third branch is called *Conservative Judaism*. The practices of the Conservative Jews are somewhat between those of Orthodox and Reform Jews. Their beliefs generally are closer to those of Orthodox Jews than to those of Reform Jews. They celebrate all the Jewish festivals. They say the Law must not be discarded but, like the Reform Jews, they adjust and change the Law to fit in with modern conditions of life. They publish study guides for women's groups and young people's groups, and have a prayer book in Hebrew and the language of the country in which they live.

The faith of the Jews is that God revealed himself and his purpose to them. The Jews believe themselves to be "God's people." Every Jewish family, anywhere in the world, is expected to keep this belief alive through family religious celebrations. To the Jews home life is especially important. In the family Jewish children learn what it means to be a Jew. Their religious laws, called the *mitzvoth*, or "precepts," were designed, Jews say, to perfect their character. They form a true bond between God and man. A Jew who truly loves the Law shows it in his character. He is kind and charitable and has a warm feeling for all people.

The religion of the Jews reminds them that they belong to one another, as people of one great tribe belong to one another. At the same time, they believe that Judaism is God's witness to all nations and all peoples, that through Judaism God speaks to the whole world.

▼   Tablets representing the Ten Commandments and the Star of David are included in the exterior decoration of this new synagogue (USA).

VIII
Christianity

Looking for the Messiah

Galilee was a small, hilly province at the northern end of the historic land of the Hebrew people, not far from the eastern shores of the Mediterranean Sea. Among its hills lay the small town of Nazareth. This town was the home of one whose life has changed the lives of millions of people. His name was *Jesus*. The calendar used by much of the world today is dated approximately from the time of his birth.

Jesus was born when Galilee, with Samaria and Judea, was part of the Roman Empire which stretched from Syria to Britain, from Germany to Ethiopia. As Jesus grew he learned the family trade of carpentry. His boyhood must have been like that of any other Jewish boy. On Friday evening, at sunset, when a blast on the ram's horn announced the beginning of the sabbath, the Jewish day of worship, he would go with his father and brothers to the synagogue. He would go again with his entire family the following morning. On other days of the week he probably studied in the synagogue school. Although he spoke *Aramaic*, the language of his people, Jesus learned to read and write in Hebrew so that he could read the

129

Jewish scriptures. He studied the words of the great prophets. He memorized the laws of his people. From the rabbis, his teachers, he learned why his people were a special people.

"God chose the Hebrew people with a plan in mind," the rabbis said. "He chose them to make his law and his rule known to the whole world." The rabbis said that some day God would send a noble leader who would make the Jews a great nation. The Jews looked forward to the coming of this leader. They called him the Messiah, the one anointed by God. Many expected that the Messiah would come soon.

The boy Jesus often thought about the Messiah. The rabbis said, "The prophet Isaiah promised that the whole world will have peace when the Messiah comes." To most Jews, however, the time of peace and happiness did not seem to be very near. Their country was not free. Their king was a puppet of the Roman emperor. Roman soldiers occupied the land and the Jews grumbled about paying taxes to a foreign power. "But all this will be changed when the Messiah comes," they declared.

Some Jews belonged to a revolutionary movement. They said, "We won't bow to anyone except to God. We won't pay taxes to any power except to our temple in Jerusalem." These Jews wanted to rebel against Rome in order to be ready for the Messiah. They were called *Zealots*.

Some Jews left their homes and lived together in small communities, often in the desert. They said, "Let us get away from the world. If we conscientiously carry out all our religious laws we will be ready for the Messiah. And he will come. Just wait!" They were called *Essenes*.

There were other Jews who tried to keep all the religious laws in the scriptures and all the traditions that had grown up around them. Their teachers spent much time studying the Law and discussing its meaning. They felt that keeping rules and customs was more important than any work a man could do. They waited for God to establish his all-powerful kingdom in Jerusalem. They were called *Pharisees*.

There were Jews who said, "We might as well get along with the

Romans. They are powerful and can preserve order in our land." The Romans allowed the temple priests to be chosen from this group. They were religiously conservative people who were comfortable and well off and not too eager for the Messiah to come. They were called *Sadducees*.

Jesus knew about these groups. He felt, however, that most people misunderstood God's purpose. To Jesus, God was like a wise and kind father, to be obeyed and respected, loved and trusted. In his view, the Zealots were impatient and did not really trust God, and the Essenes were running away from the world. Many of the Pharisees appeared to be quite religious, yet Jesus did not feel that they showed the good-will and love for people that God wanted. The Sadducees believed in keeping God's laws but had little concern for the needs of people.

A New Life

John was Jesus' cousin. John was so sure the Messiah was coming soon that he urged the Jews to get ready for him. The report went out: "John says the Messiah is coming! John says he will soon be here! John says it will be a great day for those who are ready for the Messiah but a terrible day for those who are not! John is warning us to change our way of living!" Those who listened and vowed to live clean, unselfish lives, John immersed in the waters of the Jordan River. This immersion, called a *baptism,* was a symbol of the new lives they intended to lead. Old sins had been washed away, and from then on their lives would be clean. They called John "the Baptist," that is, "the baptizer."

Jesus was about thirty years old when he heard John preach. He asked John to baptize him in the Jordan. The world is still talking about what followed. Jesus never went back to the carpenter shop.

Many think that Jesus' boyhood must have been a quiet preparation for bringing God's message to the world. One recorded that, after his birth—which took place in the small town of Bethlehem in Judea —his parents took him to the temple in Jerusalem to dedicate him to

God. His mother and father must have told him about it many times. Jesus always felt that God was very real and very close to him. One of the stories about Jesus tells of a trip his family made to Jerusalem when he was twelve years old. When it was time to go home no one knew where he was. His parents searched everywhere. At last, they found him in the temple listening to the teachers and asking them questions. Jesus was surprised that his parents had not immediately thought of looking for him in the temple. He said, "Did you not know you would find me in my Father's house?"

When Jesus was baptized by John he felt the power of God's spirit flowing through him. He felt the time had come for him to tell his people what he was certain was God's message to them!

Jesus went to a lonely place in the country to be alone, to think, and to pray in preparation for his mission. Jesus wanted to be sure to proclaim his message as God wished him to. He was tempted, at first, to gain a following by feeding the hungry and by being a benefactor of the people. He was tempted to do something startling to attract attention such as jumping from the top of the temple. He was tempted to use his abilities to obtain political power to bring the nations to God. Jesus put all these temptations out of his mind, however. He knew the only way he could show people what God is like would be to live among them, teach, let them see God's love in his life.

Jesus was now ready to begin his mission. He went back to Nazareth, to the synagogue in his hometown, and at the sabbath service read his purpose from the book of Isaiah:

> The Spirit of the Lord is upon me,
>> For he has consecrated me to preach the good news
>>> to the poor,
>> He has sent me to announce to the prisoners their release
>>> and to the blind the recovery of their sight,
>> To set the down-trodden at liberty,
>> To proclaim the year of the Lord's favour![1]

[1] Tr. Edgar J. Goodspeed (Luke 4:18).

132

Then he announced to his friends and neighbours, "This passage of Scripture has come true today." This would be his work from now on.

The Good News

Jesus went to the towns and villages, across the fields, by the shores of the lake, along the dusty roads, through the markets, wherever there were people. Often he heard them sigh and say, "Surely things will be better soon. God will send a Messiah who will be our king. Our kingdom will be God's kingdom. He will destroy our enemies."

Jesus said, "Why are you waiting around for the kingdom of God? Change your way of living! Live in God's way now! The kingdom of God is not God doing what we want him to do. It is our doing what God wants us to do." The kingdom of God is another way of saying the "rule of God." "The rule of God is coming," Jesus said. "It may come suddenly, when least expected." Jesus also said it was very near, and people needed to fit into it. Once he even said, "The rule of God is already among you." The important thing about the kingdom of God to Jesus was having faith in God and behaving toward others with the goodness of God.

Jesus often illustrated his teachings with *parables*—stories drawn from everyday life that point up an important truth. He told many parables about the kingdom of God. He told one about a king who gathered his people together and divided them into two groups the way a farmer might separate his sheep from his goats. The one group he invited to share the riches of his kingdom. The other group he threw out. Those who were invited into the kingdom were the ones who had helped people in need—fed the hungry, cared for the sick, visited those in prison—wherever they were. Those who were thrown out were the ones who had lived only for themselves.

Jesus frequently taught that God intended people to live new lives, not for themselves, but for God. Anyone, he said, who forgets himself in living as a follower of Jesus will find himself.

Jesus called for faithfulness to God and concern for one's fellow human beings. He said, "The greatest of all laws are 'You shall love the Lord your God with all your heart and with all your soul and with all your mind and with all your strength' and 'You shall love your neighbour as yourself.' "

A lawyer asked Jesus, "Who is my neighbour?" In answer, Jesus told about a man who had been beaten by robbers and left to die by the roadside. Two men passing by saw him lying there but did not help. A third man, a despised foreigner, came along and stopped to help him. He bandaged the man's wounds and took him to a place where he could be cared for. He even paid for his care. "Who proved to be a neighbour to the man in need?" asked Jesus.

"The man who cared for him," answered the lawyer.

"Go and do the same for anyone who is in need," commanded Jesus.

Jesus wanted people to understand God as Father. He wanted them to trust him and come to him. This, of course, would mean turning away from their own selfish ways. Jesus told a parable about a young man who asked for the money he would some day inherit from his father. He left home and spent it all having a good time. When his money was gone he found work keeping a farmer's pigs. He was disgusted with himself for what he had done. With no friends left and almost nothing to eat, he thought of his father. "I will go home and tell my father how sorry I am that I have done wrong," he said. "I will ask him to make me one of his servants. I do not deserve to be his son."

The father had never given up hope that some day his son would come home. The day he saw his son coming down the road, he ran to meet him. "Father, I am ashamed," said the son. But his father welcomed him with joy. "Let us celebrate," he said, "for my son who was lost is home again."

Jesus said the father's love for his son is like God's love for every human being.

Some of Jesus' most famous teachings are known as the *Beatitudes*. Beatitude comes from a Latin word that means "happy." Jesus said:

"Happy are the people who feel the need of God, for the kingdom of God belongs to them.

"Happy are those who have sorrow, for God will comfort them and give them courage.

"Happy are those who have a gentle spirit, for the whole earth will belong to them.

"Happy are those who are hungry and thirsty for goodness, for they will have it.

"Happy are those who show mercy, for mercy will also be shown to them.

"Happy are those who are completely sincere, for they will see God.

"Happy are those who make peace, for they will be called sons of God."

In the life Jesus lived, people saw what he meant by the goodness of God. They could see that he cared about them, and so they brought their troubles to him. They could see that he loved them, and so they came to him with their diseases and went away well. He used no magical ceremonies but said it was their faith that had made them well. People said, "He gets rid of demons. Surely this means he has the power of God." He assured people who were sorry for their wrongdoings that God forgave them.

Jesus spent many hours in prayer. Sometimes he prayed all night. He prayed to find out what his Father wanted him to do. Then he went out to preach to the crowds. He called them to follow him in doing God's will.

Of the many who followed him, Jesus chose twelve who were to be his closest companions. They were his first disciples. *Disciple* means "learner."

Jesus wanted his disciples to learn of God's love and God's kingdom. He wanted them to be able to carry on his work after him.

135

Enemies

Jesus openly condemned those whose religion was pretence; and he condemned those who were careful to keep religious rules and regulations but were careless of their neighbours' needs. He condemned those who took advantage of others. Those he condemned for shame and exploitation did not like him. Some Pharisees said he was against religion, that he did not keep all the religious laws. They grumbled that he spent his time with some of the worst people in the towns he went through. Some Sadducees did not like him because he was popular with the people. They were afraid he was undermining their leadership.

There was a plot to get rid of him. A large part of the record of Jesus' life, repeated and written down by his followers, tells about his last days on earth. It was the time of the Jewish Passover festival. Jesus celebrated the Passover supper in Jerusalem with his disciples. He had a long, last talk with them. He told them he would be arrested and put to death, but would rise again. He told them to remember him whenever they had a meal together, eating bread and drinking wine as a symbol of his suffering and death.

After the supper Jesus went to a nearby garden to pray. Facing arrest, he prayed that he might do, not what he wanted to do, but what God wanted him to do. He was there in the garden when the soldiers came. Faking charges of insurrection, his enemies brought Jesus to the Roman governor. They threatened to report the governor to the emperor if he did not order Jesus' immediate execution. Romans executed criminals by nailing them to a cross and letting them hang there until they died. So they nailed Jesus to a cross and left him to die. Even in dying he showed a love that few people could understand. He asked God to forgive those who were putting him to death.

Jesus was buried in a garden tomb cut in a rock below the place of execution. Jesus' disciples were afraid and went into hiding. They had believed Jesus to be the Messiah who would set up a Jewish kingdom.

Instead he had preached goodwill and taught them love for their enemies. Then he had been put to death. Their dream was at an end, and their own lives were in danger.

That was on Friday evening.

Sunday morning was different. The tomb was empty! Reports circulated that Jesus was alive! Groups of his disciples reported having seen and talked with him. It was hard to believe but finally his friends no longer doubted. "He is alive!" joyously they greeted each other. "Now, he will surely establish his kingdom."

People of the Way

Jerusalem had been crowded for the Passover festival the day Jesus was put to death. Fifty days later the city was again crowded. Jews had come from many countries to celebrate Pentecost, the festival of the barley harvest. They had come not only from all parts of Judea, but from many nations east and west of Judea. They spoke many languages. Suddenly above the din a voice called out, "Fellow Jews, listen to me." It was *Simon Peter,* one of Jesus' disciples. "Jesus of Nazareth is not dead. He is alive! He is the Messiah we have been looking for. Soon he will come again and establish the kingdom we have been waiting for!"

Those who heard Peter were impressed. He was one of the people, not a priest or an intellectual. Yet he spoke commandingly and with eloquence. He reminded the Jews of the long history of waiting for God's great day among them. "That day," he said, "has come." All through history, he explained, God had been preparing for this time. Now God's purpose was being fulfilled. Jesus' resurrection had proved that death is not the end. But even more important, the resurrected Jesus had brought God's spirit among them. Now they were to live a new life.

Obviously something had happened to Jesus' followers. The book of Acts tells what preceded Peter's sermon on the day of Pentecost.

137

For ten days Jesus' close friends and followers had been praying together in an upstairs room in Jerusalem, when suddenly, on the day of Pentecost, they felt themselves swept by a surging wind, the Spirit of God, they said, his power and his presence among them.

What happened to Jesus' followers on that day was contagious. Many who heard them believed.

The Jewish religion had always looked ahead to the great days that would come. Now it seemed the great days were near. Those who believed left their homes and lived together. They owned everything in common and shared all they had. They spent their time in the temple talking about the goodness of God and about their faith that Jesus was the Messiah and would soon be coming back. Their leaders were called *apostles,* "ones sent." They were those who had been especially close to Jesus. Those who joined the group of Jesus' followers were called "People of the Way."

The enemies of Jesus, however, were not through with his followers. The religious leaders imprisoned Peter and another apostle named *John* (not John the Baptist). A crowd mobbed and lynched a new convert, *Stephen.* The local king, *Herod Agrippa I,* ordered *James,* the brother of John, put to death.

All followers of Jesus were in danger. A few stayed in Jerusalem. Others fled for safety to the desert or to distant cities and towns. "This," thought the religious leaders in Jerusalem, "is the end of the People of the Way." Nevertheless, the more the People of the Way were persecuted, the stronger they became. Wherever they went, they told whomever they met, "We have found the Messiah. His name is Jesus. He was crucified, but he is alive again. His Spirit is among us." Many who heard them believed and joined them. When Jesus did not come back straight away his followers concluded that his return would mean something more, something far greater than just setting up a kingdom in Jerusalem.

A New Person

Saul, a Jewish student from Tarsus (now in modern Turkey), hated the People of the Way. He had tried to please God by keeping all the religious laws and traditions of the Jews. Now the People of the Way were saying that keeping all the regulations was not so important to God as acting toward people as Jesus did. Saul looked on while a mob stoned Stephen to death. "He deserves it," Saul thought. But when he heard Stephen ask God to forgive his murderers as Jesus had done, Saul could not understand. By Saul's standards Stephen should have fought back. Nor could Saul forget the look on Stephen's face as he died. God had seemed very close to Stephen.

Saul was still determined to wipe out the followers of Jesus. Armed with warrants for their arrest, he set out for the old city of Damascus in Syria. Before he arrived, however, Saul had an experience that completely changed the purpose of his life. It was as sudden as a blinding flash of light. Years later he told about it. "A voice spoke to me," he said. "It was the voice of Jesus." He tried to explain what had happened. "It was as though I, Saul, had been killed on the cross with Jesus. Saul was no longer interested in Saul. The old Saul had died. I live now only for Jesus the Christ, the Messiah. Or rather, Jesus Christ came alive in me."

From then on Saul was a different person. Writing about it later he said, "At once I went off to Arabia." In Arabia he must have spent time in thought, prayer, and study. Three years later, he wrote, after stopping again in Damascus, he visited Peter in Jerusalem and then returned to his home to preach the faith he had formerly tried to destroy. *Barnabas,* another of Jesus' followers, found Saul in Tarsus and took him to the city of Antioch in northern Syria, near Asia Minor. There he found the followers of Jesus were called *Christians.* It was a good name for them because they were followers of Jesus, the Christ, the Messiah.

The Christians of Antioch sent Saul out to tell others about Christ. He began to use his Roman name, *Paul*. The rest of his life he travelled up and down the Roman Empire declaring, "In Jesus Christ we see God's plan being completed. God not only created people, he has made it possible for people to know they belong to God as children belong to their father." Unflinchingly he faced the hardships the other Christians faced. He was persecuted by both Jews and Gentiles. Saul the persecutor had become Paul the persecuted.

Paul went west through the cities of Asia Minor to Macedonia (now in the northern part of modern Greece), to the cities of southern Greece, and to Rome in Italy. When he preached, people believed. When he moved to another city he left behind him a new *church*. "Church" was the word used for an assembly, a getting together, of God's people. They came together in each other's homes, on the banks of a stream, or wherever they could find a place to meet.

These Christians had many questions and many problems. Sometimes they wrote their questions to Paul, and he answered them in long letters. "If we die we won't be with Christ when he comes back," they worried. "Death has no victory over us," Paul replied. "Whether we live or die God will make it possible for us to be with him. Death is not the end of life."

In a later letter, which he wrote to Christians in Rome, Paul explained further, "You must not think of God's kingdom as a place on earth where people feast and drink together. God's kingdom is living in God's way." Another early Christian spoke of this as eternal life. Eternal life does not mean merely life after death. It means God's life among his people—it never ends.

The great hope (called *salvation*) in the teachings of Paul and other early Christians was for people to come together in the spirit of Jesus Christ in love for God and one another. The great evil (called *sin*) was for people to live in a way that would separate them from God and from God's love for all people.

Paul's letters were full of practical advice. "A Christian," he said, "is like a runner in a race. A good runner never looks back. He presses on toward the goal. The Christian's goal is carrying out God's purpose in his life."

"Keep your body and mind clean," he wrote. "They belong to God. You are God's temple.

"We cannot keep God's love to ourselves. It is a debt we owe to the world. We must tell everyone about Christ.

"When Christians come together and eat together in friendship and fellowship, they should remember that Christ died for them. In fact, Christians should always be living in the spirit of Christ. For those who belong together in loyalty to Christ there can be no separation and no ill feeling between them."

Paul, like many other Christians, was imprisoned and finally put to death for his faith. Even while he was in prison he never stopped telling people about Christ and writing letters to the People of the Way.

Christian Scriptures

The scriptures of the Jews became part of the Christian's *Bible*. Christians called them the *Old Testament*. When the first Christians met together they read from the Jewish books, especially the book of the prophet Isaiah. They said Jesus' life perfectly fitted Isaiah's picture of the Messiah. They sang together from the book of *Psalms*, the hymn-book of the Jews. They composed Christian songs. One of the Christians collected Paul's letters, copied them and circulated them among the churches. The letters gave such practical advice on Christian behaviour and such sensible answers to troublesome questions, that they were frequently read by Christians along with the Jewish scriptures.

Other Christians wrote down all the teachings of Jesus they could remember. A man called *Mark* wrote a book about Jesus and included many of Jesus' teachings. He wrote especially of Jesus' arrest, trial, crucifixion, and resurrection.

Two other Christians wrote books known as *"Matthew"* and *"Luke."* These writers borrowed stories from the book of Mark and used collections of Jesus' teachings that some of his followers had made. Matthew and Luke added stories about the birth of Jesus which, through the centuries, have been favourite stories of Christians everywhere. These stories, called the *Christmas* stories, say that Jesus' mother was Mary but he had no earthly father. The books of Matthew and Luke, like Mark's, are *gospels*. Gospel means "good news." Later a fourth gospel appeared called by the name "*John.*" It explains the meaning of Jesus' life and teachings. Matthew, Mark, and Luke tell about Jesus as the Messiah whom the Jews were expecting. John explains that Jesus was the expression of God's love.

Other Christians wrote letters, sermons, and tracts to answer questions about their faith, or to help Christians with their problems, and to encourage them to be strong in times of persecution. Many of these writings, such as Paul's letters, say that faith in Christ makes it possible for people to live a new kind of life, free from selfishness and pettiness.

About 350 years after Jesus' life on earth, Christian leaders recognized twenty-seven of the writings as authentic books about Jesus and the Christian way. They put the books together and called them the *New Testament*. Since that time, Christians have read and studied the Old Testament of the Jews and the New Testament of the early followers of Jesus. These two testaments form the Christians' Bible.

Turning the World Upside Down

There were many religions in the Roman Empire. They existed side by side. Anyone could belong to any religion he chose. No one interfered with another person's beliefs so long as those beliefs did not lead him to rebel against government edicts.

But Christians were different. They had to share their faith as the only faith. They had to be missionaries. That is the way the church had come into existence. Early Christians felt that the church was God's agent to carry out his purpose. His purpose was to bring the world together in his love.

That is why the church was persecuted. The Christians said, "There is only one God. He is like Christ and not like any other idea of God nor like any wooden or stone image made to represent God." Christians refused to take a loyalty oath to the emperor and bow to his statue. "That would be putting the emperor in the place of God!" they said. Christians refused to take part in any practices of their neighbours which they considered immoral or dishonest. They invited their neighbours to become Christians.

"Strange ways these Christians have," thought the officials of Rome. "We would be better rid of them." From time to time during the next 250 years there were periods of harsh persecution when Roman rulers put hundreds of Christians to death.

In spite of persecution the church grew and spread. It spread to southern and western Europe, northern Africa, and throughout Asia Minor. It was found in Persia, the land of the Zoroastrians, and in India, the land of the Hindus. Christians used a Greek word, *catholic,* when they talked about their church. Catholic meant that their faith and their church were "universal," spread throughout the world. It meant that their faith and their church were for everyone. So active were they in sharing their faith, that in one city they were accused of turning the world upside down.

In A.D. 313, the Roman Emperor *Constantine* stopped all persecution and made Christianity a legal religion. Christians were then free to worship as they pleased.

The early Christians met together in homes or by the sides of streams or sometimes, when they were being persecuted, in secret places such as the underground burial tunnels in Rome. They sang together, read the scriptures together, and shared their food together in a fellowship meal as a symbol of God's love, and their love for one another.

Growing and Changing

As time went on more and more order was brought into the service or worship. Older, mature Christians, called *presbyters* or *elders,* "older ones," guided the life of the congregations. One of the presbyters might be called a *bishop* or "superintendent." As the congregations increased, more bishops were appointed. There were bishops in all the towns and cities. The church considered the bishops of Rome (in Italy), Constantinople (now called Istanbul, in Turkey), Alexandria (in Egypt), Jerusalem (in Judea), and Antioch (in Syria) the most important bishops. The bishops of these five areas were called *patriarchs,* that is, "ruling fathers." Other bishops consulted them when their congregations had difficult questions.

The early Christians made sure that no one should be called a Christian until he understood his faith. Older Christians instructed new converts in the faith. When he was ready, a convert was baptized. Baptism was a symbol that his old life was buried and that he was rising into a new life. The new Christian declared his faith in simple words: "Jesus Christ is Lord." Later, this was expanded to, "I believe in God, the Father. I believe in Jesus Christ. I believe in the Holy Spirit."

Christians use the word *Trinity* for this triple description of God. In the early days of Christianity an actor on a Roman stage, although he remained the same actor, might use different masks for different purposes. The Latin word for mask is *persona* from which we get the English word "person." "There is one God," said the Christians, "but it is through his three masks or persons that we understand him. We know him as the one God who loves all his creatures as a good father loves his children—whose love for the world is seen in Jesus Christ, his son in a special way, whose Spirit present among his people makes them God's people, and unites them in his love."

This trinitarian or triple statement of faith became known as a *creed.* Creed comes from the Latin word *credo,* "I believe." Christians in many different places prepared their own creed statements for converts often adding long paragraphs to explain each part of the belief. They found these were not always the same, so leading Christians met together in church councils to work out creeds that Christians everywhere could use. The creeds they agreed upon expressed Christians' belief that God was creator of all things, that Jesus Christ was his son who had come from God to bring people into fellowship with God, that Jesus' mother was Mary, that he was crucified but rose from the dead and returned to God and would come again to judge all mankind. They expressed belief in God's presence or "Holy Spirit" in the world, belief that the church was universal, belief in a fellowship which bound all Christians together, belief in God's forgiveness of sins, and in life after death.

The church councils particularly wanted to explain the person of Jesus. Was he a man? Was he God? Was he both? Or neither? Some Christians emphasized his humanity, some his divinity. Some said he was only a man inspired by God. Others said he was God on earth and not a man at all. But the majority claimed he was both God and man. That is what most Christians mean today when they say they believe in the divinity of Jesus Christ. The church has always said, however, that it is really impossible to explain in words the mystery of what took place to make Jesus Christ so vital in the lives of all who put their faith in him.

New Way, New Ideas

Gradually, a few Christians, especially in Egypt, left their homes to become hermits. They believed the world was hopelessly sinful, and that good religion meant living lives of simplicity and hardship. They lived alone in caves or crude huts, ate little and slept on the ground. They owned nothing.

From the fourth century on many Christian men and women banded together in small communities for prayer and work. The men lived as monks in monasteries and the women as nuns in convents. They took vows to remain poor, to remain unmarried, and to obey the rules of the monastery or convent. It was a time when invading tribes were destroying much of the old civilization. Monks in many monasteries, however, preserved the Bible and other ancient writings, making copies by hand. One monk, *Jerome,* translated the Bible from Hebrew and Greek into Latin. It was a time when many Christians forgot that to be a Christian meant to be a witness of the Christian faith. Monks carried Christianity to France, Germany, and the British Isles.

Greater and greater numbers of people were coming into the church. There were not enough leaders to instruct them properly, and many of their old ideas crept into Christianity. Christians had once worshipped in homes or in plain buildings, but now they began to build large and beautiful churches. Worship was once the simple act of singing psalms, praying together, reading scripture passages and hearing about Jesus, but now this gave way to elaborate rituals with priests to conduct them. The word *saints* had once meant all Christians, but now it began to mean outstanding Christians, many of whom had been martyred. Statues of saints were placed in the churches. Christians had once honoured only God and Jesus, but now they began to honour Mary, the mother of Jesus, and to call her the Mother of God. The Lord's Supper had once been a time for Christians to remember Jesus and God's love as they shared a meal together, but now it also became the "miracle of the mass." Christians were saying that the bread and wine, through a miracle, became the body and blood of Christ.

The Roman Catholic Church

The bishop in Rome began to call himself the *Pope* which meant "papa." One of the bishops of Rome, Leo the Great (around 390-461), proclaimed that Peter had been the chief apostle of Jesus and had started the church in Rome. Therefore, this made the bishop of Rome chief of all the bishops.

▲ From a balcony Pope Paul VI blesses the people in St. Peter's Square, Rome.

▼ Holy Trinity Church, Stratford-on-Avon, England.

▼ African boy rings the church bell.

The church with its centre in Rome became known as the *Roman Catholic Church*. This was another way of saying, "the universal church with its headquarters in Rome." Today, there are Roman Catholic Churches around the world. Roman Catholics believe, as most other Christians do, in the Trinity. They give great honour to Mary, the mother of Jesus. They say she is in heaven and is always ready to hear the requests of people. She takes their requests to her son, Jesus. Roman Catholics also make petitions to saints asking them to take their prayers to God. Saints, Roman Catholics say, lived so close to God on earth that in heaven they are in a favoured position to bring to God the requests of worshippers. In churches and homes of Roman Catholics are images of Mary, Jesus, and the saints. Roman Catholics believe that there is a place where people go after death when they are not yet good enough for heaven but not bad enough for hell. This place is called *purgatory*. Here people are purged of their sins and made ready for heaven. Roman Catholics believe that God, through the priests, forgives sins, the wrongdoings of people that separate them from him. They believe that the bread and wine in the Lord's Supper, called the *Holy Eucharist,* becomes the body and blood of Jesus Christ in the mass, the main act in Roman Catholic worship. The mass, the Roman Catholic Church says, is the recalling of the death and resurrection of Jesus. Roman Catholics believe that the traditions of the church have considerable authority, and that only the church can interpret the meaning of the Bible. They believe that the Pope is the representative of Christ on earth and that when he speaks in this capacity, he cannot be wrong in defining a doctrine of the church. For many centuries the mass was chanted in Latin by the priests. Today, part of the mass is said in the language of the people.

Orthodox Churches

The churches in the East looked on Constantinople as a major Christian centre. Constantinople was an ancient city on the edge of

Greece situated on the strait which divides Europe from Asia. The Christians in eastern Europe respected the patriarch of Constantinople.

The bishop of the church in Constantinople did not believe the bishop of Rome had authority over him. When church councils met and made decisions Eastern churches made these decisions a basis for discussion. Western churches, however, made them church laws. The final break between the bishops of the East and the bishop of Rome came in 1054. From then on Christians in the East called their churches *Orthodox Churches*. They called themselves Orthodox because they considered their church true to early Christian beliefs. Each nation in the East had its own Orthodox Church. They still do. There are Greek Orthodox, Russian Orthodox, and Rumanian Orthodox Churches, and so on.

Worship in Orthodox Churches is a long elaborate pageant. Music sung by the choir, and chants and responses by the priests and the choir, give the worshipper a feeling of the awe and mystery of his faith. The Orthodox service represents the crucifixion and resurrection of Jesus Christ. In churches and homes of Orthodox Christians are many representations of Jesus, Mary, and the saints. Some are paintings in which the figures seem to be flat. Others are carved figures slightly raised from their background. They do not look quite real, and they are not supposed to look real because they represent, not people, but ideas. They are called *icons*. Icons are symbols of religious ideas.

Orthodox Christians call Mary the Mother of God. They say the Holy Spirit changes the bread and wine of the Lord's Supper into the body and blood of Jesus Christ. They believe Jesus gave equal power to all his apostles, that Peter was no greater than the others; therefore, the bishop of Rome cannot claim to be head of all the bishops.

Other Ancient Churches

There are other, smaller, but very ancient branches of the Christian Church. Their centre is neither Rome nor Constantinople.

Nestorian Christians are still found in Syria, north of ancient Judea. Nestorians took Christianity to Persia, to India, and, in the seventh century, to China.

Coptic Christians live in Egypt and Ethiopia.

Syrian Orthodox Christians accept the leadership of the patriarch in Antioch, Syria.

There are *Armenian Orthodox* Christians. They and the Coptic Christians claim to be the oldest branches of the Christian Church.

All of these churches differ from the Roman Catholic and the Greek Orthodox Church mainly in their understanding of Jesus' relationship to God.

Protestant Churches

There came a time in Western Europe (about the twelfth century) when people began to ask questions about their church and their faith. In France, *Peter Waldo,* a rich merchant, was disturbed that many priests and bishops had let the church become corrupt. He said that anyone who felt the spirit of Christ in his heart could preach the gospel. About the year 1170, Peter Waldo sold his business and gave his wealth to the poor. He went out to preach that God's spirit in a man's heart would help him know what was right and what was wrong. He did not have to depend on priests to tell him what to do.

In England, a priest named *John Wycliffe* (1320-1384) said that everybody needed to know what was in the Bible. He translated the Bible into English and sent out monks to read it to the people. He declared that the bread and wine in the mass did not change into the body and blood of Christ.

In Czechoslovakia, a university professor, *John Huss* (1369-1415), claimed that popes were not always right. He declared that Christians do not need popes and priests to tell them what to believe. They can know the truth by reading the Bible for themselves.

These men, and others like them, wanted to reform the church.

They wanted to make it more like the early church. They said that Christians should read and study the Bible for themselves.

Roman Catholic Church leaders considered that these men were wrong and that their ideas should be stopped. They persecuted the followers of Peter Waldo. They condemned John Wycliffe. They put to death John Huss.

The reformers' ideas were not stopped. In Germany, a monk and priest, *Martin Luther* (1483-1546), started a reform movement that spread all over Europe. Luther was a forceful man, eager to clear the church of unchristian practices that had developed in it and to awaken Christians to the meaning of Christian faith. He pointed to the teachings of Paul's letters. "Faith in God as a Father is the heart of Christian belief," he said. "You can't buy God's favour and forgiveness for your wrongdoing. You can't even work for it by good deeds," he told the people. "You need only to come to God as to a father, tell him you are sorry for your disobedience, and trust him. Gratitude for his love will make you want to do good." Luther declared that the popes and councils of the Roman Catholic Church had sometimes made mistakes and had contradicted themselves. Therefore, he said, every Christian must believe the Bible as it speaks to him, unless he can be convinced by reason that he has misunderstood what he has read.

John Calvin (1509-1564), a French priest, read the writings of Luther and became convinced that people did not understand the New Testament. He said religion was not a one-day-a-week duty but an obligation to live seven days a week according to the commandments of God. He made Geneva, in Switzerland, his headquarters. Geneva had been a city notorious for its drinking, its gambling, and its bad morals. Calvin enforced strict rules of conduct. Stern punishment was given to those whose moral conduct or religious beliefs failed to meet his code. Geneva became a city to which persecuted Protestants came and from which they carried his teachings to other countries.

The reformers did not originally intend to leave the Roman Catholic

Church but to "reform" it. The opposition of church leaders forced them and their followers into separation from those who continued to accept the full leadership of the pope. New branches or *denominations* (meaning "names") of the church sprang up in Europe. They became known as Lutheran, Reformed, Anabaptist, Mennonite, Evangelical, and by other names. Some became national churches such as the Church of Scotland. All together these churches were called Protestant Churches. *Protestant* comes from two Latin words "for" and "witness." The Protestants were witnesses for their faith. They claimed to have no rule but the Bible.

Protestants believe every Christian has the right and duty to read and interpret the Bible for himself. He does not need a priest or minister to tell him what to believe. Protestants say that since every Christian can go directly to God in prayer there is no need to call on saints or Mary to help them. They believe forgiveness of sins comes directly from God without the aid of a priest. They believe that the Bible, and not the church, is the final authority for every Christian. Most Protestants think of the Lord's Supper (sometimes called the *Communion Service*) as a time for remembering Jesus' death and his resurrection, and as a reminder of God's forgiveness of sins and the fellowship of all Christians. Protestant church services are always in the language of the people, and the members have a large say in governing their churches.

Churches such as the Church of England (in America called the Protestant Episcopal Church) and later the Old Catholic Church, which was started in Germany, and the Polish Catholic Church, and the Independent Church of the Philippines, rejected the leadership of the pope but kept many of the teachings and ways of worship of the Roman Church. Among branches of the Protestant Church are Presbyterian (Reformed), Baptist, Congregational (in America, now a part of the United Church of Christ), Friends (Quakers), Methodist, Disciples of Christ (Christian), and Pentecostals.

Like the branches of a great tree Christian churches branched off from a central trunk of early Christianity. They are united, however, in their faith in Christ and in their use of the same Bible. In their beliefs Christian churches are closer to one another than are the sects of most religions.

Sharing Their Faith

In the early days of the church, Christianity spread largely from one group of people to another. Christians told neighbours, friends, strangers, wherever they went, the good news of God's love. Merchants and travellers carried the news from one place to another. A few, like Paul, made this the total business of their lives.

When much of the world was in turmoil (about A.D. 500-1000), monks travelled widely and carried the good news to tribes and nations in Europe. In the seventh and eighth centuries, however, many nations near the Mediterranean fell before the expanding power of the *Muslims*, followers of the prophet *Muhammad*. Tens of thousands of Christians in North Africa and the Middle East became Muslims.

Later (between A.D. 1000-1500) a few Christian monks from Europe went to Muslim countries and to China to try to convert people to Christianity. They were not successful.

Although the Protestant Reformers left the Roman Catholic Church, other reformers stayed in the church and tried to clean up its corruption from within. They tried to win Protestants back to the church, and imprisoned many who would not be reconverted. They became active in taking Roman Catholic Christianity to all the world.

In the sixteenth century *Francis Xavier* (1506-1552) travelled through India saying, "You have many religions and many gods, but I have come to tell you about the one true religion and the one true God." So sure, so earnest, so powerful was Xavier that thousands in India believed him. He went to Ceylon, to islands of the East Indies, to Malaya, to Japan, and to the coast of China. Wherever he preached, thousands were converted to Christianity. Xavier promised to send

153

priests to instruct them. Many Roman Catholic priests followed Xavier and started churches in Asia. Other priests went down the coast of Africa and to North and South America. Often they tried to defend the people from mistreatment by European traders.

The Protestant Reformers were at first concerned with establishing their church on firm foundations and developing its faith. A century and a half later than Xavier, Protestants became conscious of the non-Christian countries of the world. In 1706, two German Lutheran missionaries went to India. From that time on missionaries from Germany, England, Scotland, and many of the countries of Europe travelled to India, Africa, and the Americas to preach and practice the Christian gospel.

The most famous of these men was a Baptist missionary from England, *William Carey.* Carey, a shoemaker, became a minister and went to India in 1793. He told his fellow ministers, "Expect great things from God. Attempt great things for God." He did attempt great things for his God. He supported himself and his family by his own work. Yet, the list of his accomplishments is amazing. He translated the Bible or parts of it into forty Indian languages and dialects. He started a society for the improvement of agriculture. With a fellow missionary he built a printing press on which to publish Bibles, religious books, and the first newspaper in Asia. He brought medical missions to India and started the first savings bank. He established twenty-six Christian churches and 126 Indian schools in which there were ten thousand pupils. His letters home aroused Christians in England to organize a society for sending out more missionaries.

Wherever they went, Christian missionaries built schools, colleges, and hospitals. In these acts of compassion, Christ was their example and inspiration.

Soon there were new congregations in Asia, in Africa, in the islands of the sea, all around the world. Today, these churches are sending missionaries to other parts of the world to share their faith.

Christians believe they have a mission. Their mission is to carry out God's purpose. God's purpose, they say, is to unite all people under God, their Father. Only in knowing Christ, Christians believe, can people know what God is like. Faith in Christ brings people to God. Because they believe that faith in Christ can bring people together in love and goodwill, the mission of Christians is to invite people home to God.

Roman Catholic missionaries say that "home" is the Roman Catholic Church. Theirs is the church, they believe, that Jesus Christ started. He intended that Peter, and after him the popes in succession, should represent him, they say.

Protestant missionaries say that faith in Christ is most important. They believe everyone should have the experience of knowing that Christ can save him from a life of self-centredness. Protestant missionaries want everyone to become a personal follower of Jesus Christ.

Christian Festivals

Among the many festivals that help Christians remember their Christian heritage are *Christmas, Easter,* and *Pentecost.*

Christmas is a gay festival that celebrates the birth of Jesus. Homes and streets are decorated with lights, tinsel, and evergreen trees—symbols of eternal life. The sound of music fills the air. Gifts are given, often in secret, as a way of expressing love for each other.

Easter is a joyous day that celebrates the resurrection of Jesus Christ. On this day many Christians dress in new clothes and churches are decorated with plants and flowers, symbols of new life.

Pentecost, fifty days after Easter, is celebrated as the birthday of the Christian Church.

The People of God

Christians today are talking about the "people of God." They see many people in the world who are in need, many who are in trouble,

155

many who do not know the love of God. Whose job is it to help them and to share with them God's love? Christians are answering, "It is the laymen's job." A *layman* is anyone who belongs to the church. Layman comes from a Greek word used in the New Testament for the "people" of God. The church is not the minister or the priest. It is the people of God, the laymen. So Christians today are discovering what they say the first Christians always knew: it is the job of all the people of God to live in God's spirit—that is, to be led by the Holy Spirit—and to share with others their faith in God's love.

Laymen are getting together with fellow workers to discuss their Christian faith. Some invite their neighbours into their homes to worship with them. Some become friends of boys and girls who have no father or mother, no homelife, or who are in trouble. Wherever they are, at home or in a strange land, they share with others the best that they know to share—God's love.

Many Christians are active in working out what they call "new forms of Christian living in a changing world." They are trying to find new ways of making the love that Jesus taught a vital force in all life's relationships—in crowded cities, in isolated country places, or in parts of the world where people and governments face new problems in learning to live together. It is God's plan, these Christians say, that all people live together in goodwill.

Getting Together

Bringing the whole world together in loyalty to Christ who is the expression of God's love! That is the main purpose of Christianity according to the men who wrote the Christian scriptures, the New Testament. All the history of the church contains a story of Christians' search for this fellowship. Today, Christians, although they may live in different parts of the world and worship in different ways, are finding this fellowship more than ever before. People of different denominations are meeting together for worship and the study of the Bible. They are joining together to bring relief to people in want and to resettle refugees who have lost their homes. They are working together in building schools and hospitals, in printing Christian literature, and improving agriculture in underdeveloped areas. They are thinking together about the meaning of the Christian faith and are studying ways of sharing it.

Early gatherings of Christians were called *ecumenical* councils. The meeting, studying, working, and worshipping together that is taking place between and among the various branches of the Christian Church today is called the ecumenical movement. It means all Christians working together to bring all the gospel to all the world. Some people think this is the most important development in the Christian Church in its recent history. Christians whose religion is today numerically the largest religion in the world, are declaring to the whole world that although there are many branches and many ways of worshipping within the church, there is but one church with one Lord, who is Jesus Christ, and with one message—the love of God for all people.

▼   Evangelist Billy Graham preaches in stadium in Frankfurt, Germany.

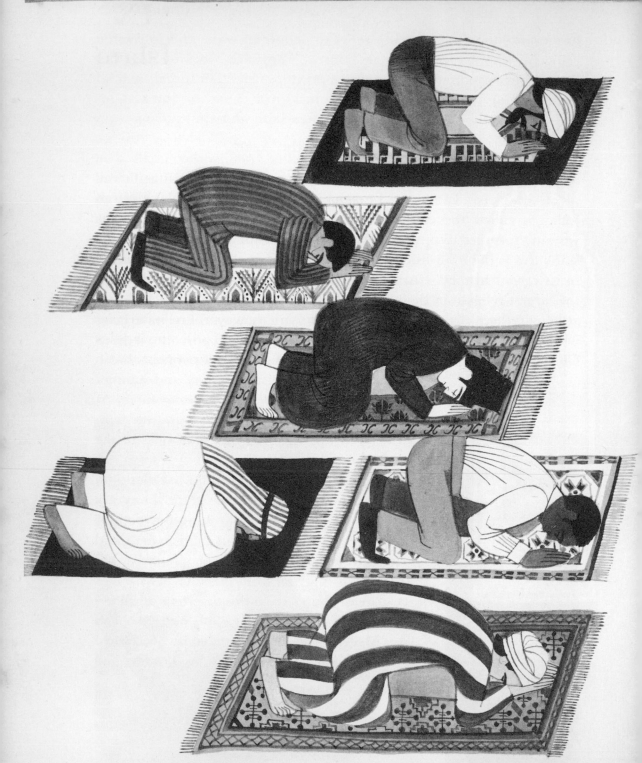

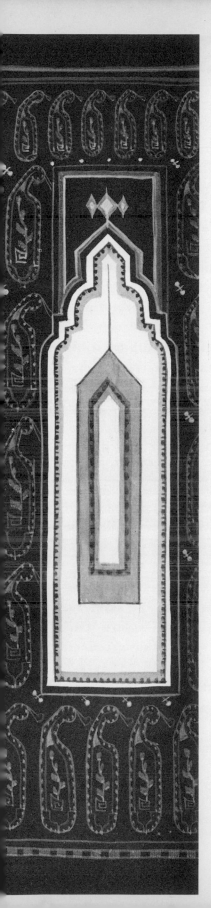

IX
Islam

The "Island of the Arabs"

The people of the Arabian Peninsula call it "The Island of the Arabs." And an island it is. It lies between the Red Sea on the west and the Persian Gulf on the east, with the deserts of Iraq and Jordan to the north and the Arabian Sea to the south. Parallel to the west coast rise high, almost inaccessible rock mountains. Here and there, however, are waterholes and, where the winter rains can collect, green oases with date palms and grass. In this harsh desert land the sun blazes by day and summer temperatures climb to 130 degrees or more. At night the sky is bright with stars, and the temperature drops in some places almost to the freezing point.

Longer than man can remember Bedouin tribes have inhabited this region. They are constantly on the move searching for food for themselves and pasturage for their camels and goats. Twenty per cent of the people in Arabia are nomads, moving from place to place.

Caravan routes cross the desert in all directions. In ancient times caravans carried spices from Mecca near the western coast northward to the city of Damascus in Syria. Traders had

159

to be constantly on the lookout for desert tribes who were ready to swoop down and rob a caravan.

The people who lived and travelled in this desert land long ago knew the harshness of nature. Each day they faced the threat of hunger and thirst. They stood in awe of nature, and feared it. They wondered, "Where does the sun get its heat and the stars their light?" They imagined that some sort of spirit inhabited each oasis, waterhole, tree, and rock. So they worshipped spirits and trees and rocks, the sun, the moon, and the stars. Each tribe also had its own gods. They had a hazy idea of some kind of high god who was in charge of everything, but he was far away and few worshipped him.

In western Arabia between the Red Sea and the mountains, tribes became a settled people long ago. They built cities and towns and carried on a spice trade with foreign nations. Mecca and Medina were centres for the spice trade.

The people of Mecca felt superior to the wandering Bedouin tribes. They were good businessmen. They knew something about people outside the "Island of the Arabs." Their spice trade with foreign nations had given them a knowledge of what was going on in the world. And in control of Mecca was the strong *Quraysh* tribe. They believed in many gods and especially in three goddesses whom they called the daughters of Allah. Allah was the name of a far-off god who had no image.

Most important of all, the people of Mecca had in their possession a holy stone, a black meteorite which had fallen from the skies, no one knew how long ago. The stone was built into a square temple which, they said, had been erected by the ancient desert chief, Abraham. They called the temple the *Kaaba* which means the "cube." Each year Bedouin tribesmen streamed across the desert to worship at the Kaaba. They sacrificed sheep or goats or camels. They thought that if they ran around the stone seven times and kissed it, the heavens would bless them. In the unlit interior of the Kaaba they worshipped a variety of idols, said to be 360, representing many gods and goddesses.

In this desert land and in this city, the youngest of the world's great religions, *Islam,* was born.

Muhammad

About A.D. 570, *Muhammad* was born in *Mecca.* No one who knew him as a child thought he would be the most famous Arab who ever lived. His father had died before he was born. His mother died when he was six years old. He lived with his grandfather for two years. When his grandfather died, his uncle, *Abu Talib,* became his guardian.

Muhammad, like other Arab boys, probably herded camels and goats. He may have gone on caravan journeys with his uncle. When Muhammad was twelve years old he went with a caravan north to Syria. There he met Christians. An old tradition says that Muhammad and a Christian monk became friends. Muhammad was impressed by the Christians' worship of only one God.

When he was twenty-five years old Muhammad went to work for a wealthy widow, *Khadijah.* She had many caravans and Muhammad journeyed with her caravans to the great cities of Syria. He saw and heard more of the world than he had ever known before. He talked with people from many places with many different ideas. He met Christians, Jews, and Zoroastrians.

Khadijah was older than Muhammad, but Muhammad fell in love with her and married her. As Khadijah's husband he no longer needed to work. He had money and leisure to sit and ponder the new ideas he had heard in his travels. Often he went to a cave outside Mecca to think about questions that troubled him. "Why do the Arabs worship many gods and the Christians and Jews only one?" he asked himself. "Why do my fellow-tribesmen use idols while for Christians and Jews the unseen God is very real without images?"

One day in the cave, Muhammad had a vision. He said an angel, *Gabriel,* appeared to him and told him of a sacred book in heaven that had been there since the beginning of time. The book, he said, was the *Koran* (sometimes written *Qur'an*). Gabriel recited some of its verses to Muhammad.

Muhammad had other visions. Gradually he came to the conclusion that he was to be the prophet of the one true God whom he called *Allah*. At first he told no one but Khadijah and Abu Talib, his uncle. Khadijah believed in Muhammad's visions. She encouraged him to go out and preach that there is only one true God to whom everyone should submit. So Muhammad began to preach Islam to the people of Mecca.

Islam means "submission." A person who submits to the will of Allah, according to the doctrines of Islam, is called a *Muslim*. Muhammad urged the Meccans to submit to Allah's will. A few listened to him and accepted his teachings. But most of the townspeople did not like Muhammad's attacks on the local gods. They persecuted his followers, and many fled to Ethiopia across the Red Sea. Muhammad's troubles increased. Khadijah and Abu Talib, his two loyal supporters, died. A plot against Muhammad's life was uncovered. The Meccans wanted nothing to do with any teachings that would do away with their idols. Muhammad decided it was time to leave Mecca. In A.D. 622 he turned his back on his birthplace and went to Medina, 220 miles to the north. (At that time the city was called Yathrib. Later it was called Medina, the "City of the Prophet.") Muhammad's flight is called the *Hegira* and marks the year one in the Muslim calendar. Time among Muslims is designated A.H.—anno (in the year of) Hegira.

The people of Mecca were glad to see Muhammad go. They thought they were at last rid of him and his visions and his bothersome teachings about one God. They went on worshipping the idols in the Kaaba undisturbed. Eight years later, however, Muhammad returned from Medina at the head of an army. He captured Mecca and cleared the idols out of the Kaaba. From then on the Kaaba with its black stone was to be the centre of Muslim pilgrimages. Until this time Muslims

◄ Kaa'ba in Mecca, centre of pilgrimage for all Muslim men. Pilgrims walk around the Kaa'ba and kiss the black stone in its wall.

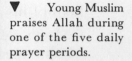
▼ Young Muslim praises Allah during one of the five daily prayer periods.

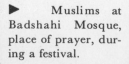
▲ Muslim reads the Koran, sacred scriptures containing the revelations to Muhammad.

► Muslims at Badshahi Mosque, place of prayer, during a festival.

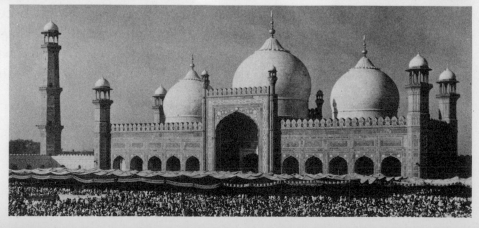

had faced Jerusalem when they prayed. After the capture of Mecca, however, a Muslim, when he prayed, faced Mecca. Muslims still face Mecca when they pray, no matter what part of the world they are in.

Muhammad had at first been only a religious leader. In Mecca he had preached to the people to submit to Allah. In Medina, however, he became not only religious leader of the city but also its military commander. His preaching inspired his followers with zeal for the worship of Allah. His laws regulated every part of their lives. With the help of his army he hoped to expand his authority and his religion over all Arabia. Muhammad wanted to bind all Arabs into one brotherhood. Because he believed Allah had called him to restore the true religion of Abraham, he had hoped Jews and Christians would accept Islam. When they did not, he turned against them.

Muhammad lived only ten years after his flight to Medina. They were ten busy years. In that time he united all the tribes of Arabia under the banner of Islam. In the century that followed, Islam spread across the land from India to Egypt. It took North Africa and Spain and almost gained a foothold in France. The Muslim armies were pushed back to Spain at the Battle of Tours in France in A.D. 732.

Six Beliefs

Every Muslim believes: there is *one* God, Allah; there are angels of God; there are holy books; there are prophets of God; Allah controls the world and history; there will be a day of judgment.

The heart of Muslim belief is that Allah is one God, all-seeing, all-hearing, all-speaking, all-knowing, all-willing, and all-powerful. Allah cannot be pictured. There are to be no images of God or of any being in God's creation. There is nothing on earth or in heaven equal to Allah. There are ninety-nine beautiful names for God. That is why Muslims often carry strings of ninety-nine beads, or strings with thirty-three beads (which can be repeated three times) for the names of God. There is a story that there are one hundred names. But Muhammad whispered the hundredth name to his camel, and the camel won't tell. That is why camels walk with such dignity across the desert. They know something no one else knows.

Muslims believe that the angels of God are holy beings created out of light. Chief of the angels is Gabriel, who appeared to Muhammad and gave him the Koran. There is a bad angel who was put out of heaven. He is called *Iblis* or *Shaitan*. There are *djinn* (sometimes written *jinn*) which are created of fire. Some djinn are helpful, but many are troublemakers.

Muslims call themselves, as well as Christians and Jews, "people of the book." The "book of books" for Muslims is the Koran. There have been four holy books, they say, the Book of the Laws of Moses (Torah), the Psalms of David (*Zabur*), the Evangel or Gospel of Jesus (*Injil*), and the Koran. The Koran, they believe, supersedes the other revelations of God. Muslims say all the other books have been corrupted. The true Injil or New Testament, they believe, was taken back to heaven by Jesus and so the New Testament Christians have today is not the real New Testament. It is, say the Muslims, only a corruption.

Koran means "recitations." It gets its name from Gabriel's command to Muhammad: "Recite, in the name of the Lord who has created." Muslims say the Koran was handed down to Muhammad over a period of twenty-three years. Muhammad himself, some say, could not read or write but recited his revelations to his followers, who wrote them down on whatever material they had at hand. When Muhammad died his followers gathered the sayings together from writings on camel bones, stone tablets, leather parchments, and from the memory of people. The collection was completed about A.D. 650. Muslims believe the Koran is an exact copy of the original Koran in heaven. It was handed down to Muhammad in *Arabic*, therefore, no translation of the Koran in other languages is the true Koran. Muslims everywhere learn and recite the Koran in Arabic. The Koran, together with the traditions, regulates the life of a Muslim from birth until death. Muslims think of the Koran as a "wonder" of God.

Muslims also have the *Hadith* or "Tradition," said to be a collection of the teachings and rulings of Muhammad. These were not revealed to Muhammad in a vision and are not part of the Koran. Many of them were added much, much later. They are important to Muslims, however, because they show them how to meet situations for which there is no instruction in the Koran.

Muslims say there have been 124,000 prophets of God although only twenty-two are mentioned in the Koran. The chief prophets were Adam, Noah, Abraham, Moses, David, Jonah, Jesus, and Muhammad. Jesus, they say, did not die on the cross. At the last minute someone was substituted for Jesus and God took Jesus directly to heaven. Muhammad is the apostle of Allah. He was the most important prophet. He was also the last prophet. Sometimes Muslims call him the "seal" of the prophets. After Muhammad, they say, prophecy—speaking for God—was "sealed up," and since then there have been no more prophets.

Everything that happens in the world has been decided by Allah beforehand, say Muslims. Nothing that anyone does can change Allah's will. This has been called the *Law of Predestination*. Some Muslim leaders say God does let people make their own decisions, but at any moment he can take control of man's activities again. This has tended to make people submit to everything that happens without struggle because it is God's will. This has been called *fatalism*.

On the Day of Judgment, Muslims say, the souls of the dead will cross a long, narrow bridge. Some will fall off into the fires of hell. Others will reach paradise. Here they will lie on silk-covered couches, in lovely gardens, by flowing rivers. They will be waited on by beautiful maidens and will eat the finest of foods. Many modern Muslim teachers say that these descriptions of paradise are symbols of a more perfect life in heaven.

Five Duties

Every Muslim is expected to perform five duties. These duties are called *Pillars of Islam* because they underlie the Muslim beliefs:

1. A Muslim must recite the creed of Islam. It is a short creed called the "word of witness." Every day a Muslim says in Arabic *"La ilāha illa Allāh, wa Muhammad rasūla Allāh."* ("There is no God but Allah and Muhammad is the apostle of Allah.") This creed must be recited aloud, perfectly, at least once in a lifetime.

2. A Muslim must say set prayers five times a day. Muslims say that one night, in a dream, the angel Gabriel took Muhammad to Jerusalem on a winged horse. There, under a rock where the Jewish temple had stood, Muhammad met the prophets of old. From the rock he ascended through all the heavens until in the seventh heaven he met Allah. Allah commanded him to have his followers prostrate themselves in prayer five times a day. In Muslim countries, a man called the *muezzin* shouts the call to prayer every day before dawn, at noon, in the afternoon, in the evening, and again at night—five times. He may give the call from the *minaret,* a tower of the *mosque* which is the Muslim place of meeting. When a Muslim hears the call he faces Mecca and recites his prayers. Before he prays he washes his feet, his hands, and his arms up to his elbows. He recites passages from the Koran. He begins his prayer in a standing position but during his prayer he also sits, kneels, and stretches himself out on the ground with his forehead on a small prayer stone. At noon on Fridays, Muslim men gather in a mosque to recite their prayers. In the mosque they are led by an *imam,* a man who is known to be religious and a scholar. The prayers of a Muslim are prayers of praise to Allah. If a Muslim cannot go to a mosque he may spread his prayer rug out wherever he is and pray. In the desert, where there is no water, he may wash with sand. Only men are required to say the set prayers.

3. A Muslim must fast in the month of *Ramadan.* Ramadan is the ninth month of the Muslim calendar. This is the month, Muslims say, in which the Koran was handed down from heaven. Fasting in Ramadan is an absolute duty. During the day no one may take a bite of food or drop of water. The Koran says nothing about the night so Muslims eat food and drink water after dusk or before dawn.

4. A Muslim must give *alms.* Muslims call the giving of alms *zakat.* An upright Muslim gives alms to help widows and orphans, the sick and the poor. The Koran says a man should give a fortieth of his money to charity. He should give a tenth of his grain and fruit if his land is well watered, but need give only a twentieth if he has to irrigate his land. In giving alms the Muslim is sharing with his brothers the abundance Allah has given to him. The Koran says, "The best and most beautiful of my creatures is a compassionate man who gives alms."

5. A Muslim must make a *pilgrimage* to Mecca. A Muslim, who can afford it and is physically and mentally able, is expected to make the pilgrimage to the Kaaba in Mecca at least once in his lifetime. Pilgrimage time is the twelfth month of the Muslim year. The ceremonies in Mecca are strenuous, and a pilgrim must be especially fit to attempt them. Pilgrims run seven times around the Kaaba, three times fast and four times slowly, as they did in the days before Muhammad. Each time they stop to kiss the black stone or to reach out and touch it, if the crowd is too great for them to get close to it.

Their next act is called the *Lesser Pilgrimage* which consists of running back and forth between two hills that face each other across a valley. This is done seven times in imitation of the mother of *Ishmael* frantically searching in the desert for water for her little son. Ishmael is said to have been the founder of Mecca and the father of the Arabs.

Then comes the *Greater Pilgrimage,* with the pilgrims going on foot to visit places important in Arabian history. This ceremony ends with the *Great Festival* when wealthier pilgrims sacrifice a goat, sheep, camel, or cow and share it with poorer pilgrims.

Merrymaking at the Great Festival lasts three days. Then the pilgrims return to Mecca to run once more around the black stone. On the pilgrimage all wear simple clothes; there is no difference between rich and poor. Hundreds of thousands make the journey to Mecca each year. When the ceremonies are over most Muslims go to Medina to visit the grave of Muhammad.

The pilgrimage to Mecca is known as the *Hajj,* and one who has made the pilgrimage is ever after called Hajj or Hajji. It is a great honor to be a Hajji.

A *jihad,* or holy war, is sometimes called the sixth pillar of Islam. A holy war is a war in the defence of Islam. The first five pillars are duties demanded of every Muslim man, but the holy war is not an obligation put on everyone.

The Muslim has a strict code of conduct. He follows rigid food laws and does not eat pork. His laws forbid him to gamble or to drink alcoholic beverages. They condemn lending money at high rates of interest. A Muslim may, if he can afford it, have as many as four wives at one time, but no more. He is expected to treat them all equally.

Islam Since Muhammad

Who was to be the leader of Islam after Muhammad's death?

One group of Muslims thought the leader should be chosen from the people who had been especially close to Muhammad, those who were called the *Companions.* Another group thought the new leader should be a descendant of Muhammad. They called themselves the *Legitimists.* Later on Muhammad's own tribe, the Quraysh tribe, said that they should decide who should be leader.

The Companions chose Muhammad's first successor. He was *abu Bakr,* Muhammad's first convert in Mecca. He had been very close to

Muhammad. Sometimes, when Muhammad was away, abu Bakr had led the prayers. Abu Bakr was leader for only one year but he accomplished much. It was he who started the collection of the sayings preserved on pieces of bone and parchment and in people's memories that make up the Koran. He subdued tribes that wanted to break away after Muhammad's death, and he followed Muhammad's plan for conquest of the world outside Arabia.

Muhammad had predicted that there would be seventy-eight break-away sects in his religion. He said they would all pass away, however, and only Islam would remain. There have been many sects but the two most important branches of Islam have been and are the *Sunni* and the *Shiah*.

The Sunnis claim to hold to the traditions of Muhammad. Sunnis are numerous in Arabia, North Africa, and the countries around the Mediterranean.

The Shi'ites (those who belong to the Shiah branch of Islam) say that Muhammad's son-in-law, *Ali,* and Ali's descendants were the rightful leaders of Islam. Ali was leader for a short time. He was murdered and his older son, *Hasan,* became the Imam or "leader." Hasan was soon forced to resign. Then Ali's second son, *Husain,* was killed in a battle when he tried to claim his right to be the Imam. Shi'ites remember this battle at their *Muharram* festival each year.

Most Shi'ites say there were twelve divinely appointed Imams who interpreted the law correctly and who never committed a sin. The last one died or disappeared in A.D. 878. The Shi'ites say that he did not die but disappeared into a cave near Baghdad which is in Iraq. Just before the last days of the world he will return. They call him the *Mahdi,* "the one guided by Allah," who will bring justice and peace to earth. Shi'ites are found mostly in Iraq, Iran, Pakistan, and India.

The *Ismailites* are a sect that grew out of the Shiah branch. They had their beginnings in a secret society in the ninth century. They are sometimes called the *Seveners* because they believe that Ismail, son of the sixth Imam, was the rightful seventh Imam. They say he did not die but was hidden and will some day return as the Mahdi.

The *Wahhabis* are one of the most zealous sects of Islam. They were organized in Arabia in the eighteenth century to bring Muslims back to the strict life Muhammad had required of his followers. The Wahhabis called for a disciplined life without indulgence. Early in the twentieth century, through a sheikh named *ibn Saud,* the Wahhabis conquered most of Arabia and set up the Saudi Arabian monarchy.

Many Muslims have for centuries looked for the coming of the Mahdi, "the one guided by Allah." From time to time men have claimed to be the Mahdi. Many have been strong leaders. In the nineteenth century a leader in the Sudan declared he was the Mahdi. He was a hard fighter and roused the fanatic devotion of thousands of Sudanese. With them he was able to defeat his enemies and set up his own rule.

In India, in 1879, *Mirza Ghulam Ahmad* claimed to be the Mahdi the Muslims were expecting, and also the Messiah of the Jews and the Christians. Ahmad said the jihad, or holy war, was not to be a military war as most Muslims thought, but a quiet conversion of people to right living. Ahmad's followers are found in the *Ahmadiya* sect. There are Ahmadiya missionaries in many parts of the world.

In 1844 a Persian Shi'ite Muslim, after he had returned from a pilgrimage to Mecca, said he was the Mahdi. He called himself *Bab-ed-Din* which means "door" or "gate" to the truth. He said that he had come to prepare mankind for the final great age on earth. Out of this movement came the *Baha'i* sect. Other Muslims say that Baha'i is not a true sect of Islam but a heresy.

A religious group called the *Black Muslims* did not come out of Islam but adopted many Islamic forms and ideas.

Lovers of God

Egypt and Persia were two of the countries which fell under Arabic conquest soon after the time of Muhammad. Most of the people became Muslims. Most of them have remained Muslims. Some of them, however, were not comfortable in Islam the way the Arabs practised it. The Egyptians had been mostly Coptic Christians. The Persians had been mostly Zoroastrians. There had been a feeling for God in their religions that they did not find in Arabian Islam. To them, the Arabs' religion seemed cold and hard.

They wanted a God who was close to them. In fact many of them said that only God is real, and the whole purpose of life is to get to God and forget this evil world. When the Egyptians and Persians became Muslims some of their ideas about God stayed with them. There were a few Egyptians and Persians who, as Muslims, said, "The whole purpose of life is to love Allah so much that we will forget ourselves and the world and lose ourselves in him." This is known as *mysticism*.

Such Muslim mystics have been called *Sufis*. Some Sufis left their homes and came together to live in their own small communities or brotherhoods. There were among the Sufis, groups of men and women known as *dervishes,* many of whom used music, drugs, dancing, and hypnotic suggestions to try to find union with God. Those who have danced or whirled until they became exhausted have been popularly called "whirling dervishes."

Muslim Festivals

Muharram, a ten-day festival, commemorates the death of Ali, a cousin and son-in-law of Muhammad, and his sons Hasan and Husain who were Muhammad's grandsons. The festival takes its name from the first month of the Islamic calendar, the month Husain and his family were killed. Since that time Shi'ites have considered Husain a martyr. They erect black tents in the streets where people in mourning clothes assemble on the first day of the festival to hear the story of Husain. They sit on the ground weeping and crying out, "Husain, Husain." During the first nine days, processions of half-naked men go through the streets beating themselves and performing wild dances. On the last day great crowds gather to watch a passion play which depicts the sufferings, death, and burial of Husain.

Sunnis celebrate only the tenth day of the month, commemorating creation. Adam and Eve, heaven and hell, life and death, they say, were created on this day.

Baqar-'Id or "the Great Festival" takes place in the month of pilgrimages to Mecca. Every Muslim who can afford it, whether he goes to Mecca or not, is required to sacrifice an animal. This reminds them of the tradition that Abraham, instead of sacrificing his son, sacrificed a sheep to God. The sacrificial animal is killed with his head pointing in the direction of Mecca. As part of the festival, prayers are said and sometimes a sermon is preached. The animal is cooked and eaten by the family, who have fasted during the preparation of the feast. The family shares its food with neighbours and with the poor.

Islam Today

Next to Christianity, Islam has more followers than any other religion in the world. Most of the people in the countries of south west Asia and in North Africa are Muslims. The largest populations of Muslims are found in Pakistan and Indonesia. There are many millions of Muslims in Malaysia, in India, and in China, and a large number in the Philippines, in the Soviet Union, in southern Europe, in west Africa, and along the coasts of east Africa. Muslims everywhere are united in their Word of Witness, "There is no God but Allah, and Muhammad is the apostle of Allah."

Islam is changing to meet the challenges of modern times. Religious leaders are reinterpreting and modernizing old teachings of Islam. Sometimes they use Christian ideas. Islam's missionary activity is having widespread influence in Asia, and especially in Africa. Islam is more active today than it has been for the past five hundred years.

X
Religions
Today

Growing

Religions are like people. Religions grow.

A baby is centred in himself and cries for what he wants. As he grows older he learns to live with other people. As he grows to be an adult he takes responsibility for other people. The most responsible type of person lives, not for himself, but for others.

The religions of tribal people often seem like the fears, imaginings, and play of small children. Religion among tribal people is the attempt to get spirits and gods to give them what they want. It is the attempt to make the spirits and gods do what they want them to do. It is behaving in such a way that spirits and gods will not punish them.

The great world religions are religions that have grown up. They still help people meet their needs. They still give people codes of conduct to help them get along with one another.

Symbols in globe, opposite page: Circles, clockwise from top—Chinese religions; Hinduism; Zoroastrian; Buddhism; Islam; American Indian (representing ancient unrecorded religions); Christianity; and Judaism. Centre, 9-point star, Baha'i; fish, Christianity; ankh, everlasting life; dove, many faiths; tablets, Judaism; lotus, Hinduism-Buddhism; water sign (Chinese), spiritual life.

They also, however, help people become more mature in the way they behave. They teach them to be responsible for the way they live their lives, responsible for the world they live in, responsible for each other. They explain what life means.

Changing and Borrowing

Growing is changing.

People keep many ideas and customs of their parents, grandparents, and ancestors. But they also develop new ideas and customs that make them different from their parents and grandparents. A grandson may look like one of his grandfathers. Then people say, "He is just like his grandfather." But he isn't really just like his grandfather, because he is a different person living in a different time. Religion in each generation is never exactly as it was in a previous generation.

People change as they grow older. So do religions. Some people become grey-haired or bald. Some grow fat. Others grow thin. An experience a person has had or a new skill he has learned may change his ways of living. His ideas change. The way he thinks about the world changes. All their lives people keep changing in one way or another. Religions are like people.

In all religions, through the generations and centuries, there are some ideas and words and ways of worship that remain the same. This is called *continuity*. Continuity is what many people like about their religion. They can believe and worship as their ancestors did. The world may change, they say, but their religion does not change.

Although a religion may keep its old ideas and old forms of worship, it does change in some ways. Religious teachers change the way they explain their faith. They do so because old explanations, like an old dialect, or the words of an old language, may no longer be understood. They do so because each new generation has new ideas, new ways of speaking, and a new understanding of the world in which it lives. Often they discover meanings in their faith which they feel have been neglected and which they wish to recover. Sometimes religious leaders are so impressed by what they have learned from science, or by what they have learned from another religion that they use some of those ideas in their own religion.

Change has gone on more rapidly in the twentieth century because the lives of people all around the world have changed more rapidly. Science, war, industry, and technology have changed their lives. They have new needs which their religions must meet. They have new questions their religions must answer.

Borrowing has gone on more rapidly in the twentieth century because the people of the world have been coming together more often and learning from each other.

Japanese Buddhists visited Protestant churches. They liked the Protestant Sunday schools, the singing, and the youth groups, and copied them. Hindus in India saw the work of Christian missions. They imitated the methods of helping people which Christian missions used. Some Christians liked the Hindu emphasis on quiet meditation. Now there are meditation centres where Christians come together to think quietly about God.

All religions have borrowed words, ideas, and explanations from each other, but mostly they have borrowed from Christianity.

No Religion?

Some people appear to have very little of any kind of religion.

Some Muslims are like Rahim. He calls himself a Muslim. Yet, he takes a drink when he can get it although his religion states that the use of alcoholic beverages is wrong. Rahim no longer goes to the mosque to pray. He has even forgotten how to make his prayers to Allah.

But other Muslims are like Abdul who joins his father and brothers in the mosque for prayers. They are sure of Allah, sure of their religion. They feel a sense of brotherhood with all other Muslims.

Some Hindus are like Lalita. He calls himself a Hindu. Yet, he eats

177

meat, although for Hindus the eating of meat is not good. Lalita does not bathe in the river or temple tank, although his religion states that he should bathe each morning. Lalita does not observe Hindu ceremonies, although his religion tells him to worship. Lalita owns a bicycle shop and has a good income. He has no time to go to the Hindu temple.

But other Hindus are like Prem Lal who stops on his way to school to worship at a shrine. He is sure that if he keeps his thoughts fixed on Brahman instead of on himself his life will be finer, his India better.

Some Buddhists are like Myint. He calls himself a Buddhist. Yet, he thinks nothing of taking food from his employer's shop, although his religion forbids stealing. He belongs to a political club that once staged a riot in which people were killed. It didn't bother Myint although his religion condemns killing. Myint does not listen to the Buddhist teachers. He never prays at a Buddhist shrine.

But other Buddhists are like Tin who has memorized parts of the Buddhist scriptures and is determined to live by their teachings. He is sure that if the whole world lived by the teachings of Gautama the Buddha, there would be no selfishness, no greed, no war in the world.

Some Christians are like Mike. He calls himself a Christian. Yet, he does not read his Bible. He does not pray. He speaks the name of God and Christ when he is angry, but he has no idea what God or Christ are really like. Mike is very busy trying to make money and to have a good time. He seldom goes to church.

But other Christians are like John who takes the teachings of Jesus seriously. He tries to live his life in such a way that the world will understand and live by God's love.

There are many people in this world like Rahim and Lalita and Myint and Mike. They say they belong to a religion, but they do not practise their religion.

There are others who do go to the Muslim mosque, or to the Hindu temple, or to the Buddhist shrine, or to the Christian church but who do not understand their religion. They live each day as Rahim, Lalita, Myint, and Mike do, as though there were no religion but themselves.

For many, their religion is themselves. They live to get the things they want. They live to do the things they please. They neglect the ideas of goodwill, unselfishness, and responsibility to others. When great numbers of people live by no religion but themselves, some new set of ideas takes the place of religion, and often a dictator government takes over to control them.

If these people had lived in ancient times they would very likely have been religious to keep the spirits or gods from punishing them. They would have been religious to get from the gods the things they wanted. But in these times they do not believe in gods and spirits. They are not afraid a god will punish them. They do not need ancient tribal religion to get what they want. They feel that they do not need a religious explanation of the world. They do not want to be bothered with mature religion that teaches them high ideals or asks them to serve others.

Such people probably like to do what everyone else is doing. If everyone else were religious they would be religious, too. When most of their neighbours are not especially concerned with religion, neither are they. They do not want their private lives interfered with by religion. They do not want their consciences to be bothered. This is sometimes called *secularism*.

Then there are people who say: "I do not have any religion because I do not know whether religion is true or not." They call themselves *agnostics*.

A few say: "All religion is untrue. There is no God." These people will not believe anything they cannot see or touch. Such people may call themselves *atheists*. Religious leaders try to help people to grow up, to give up foolish ideas about God, and to accept sensible ideas. Atheists, however, do not want to believe any ideas about God, good or bad. They say they disapprove of all religion.

New Religions

There are many new religions in the world.

There are many new religions in Africa. A new religion was started in Zululand in 1911 by *Isaiah Shembe* who called himself a prophet. The sick came to Isaiah Shembe to be made well. He performed a ceremony of purification for people who came confessing that they had done wrong and wanted to be made right. He blessed the harvests.

Shembe's religion had its roots in his many experiences with lightning. When he was a boy lightning struck near him as he was praying. It seemed to him that a voice was speaking, saying, "Stop doing wrong!" Lightning struck a second time after Isaiah had grown and married four wives. Again he heard the voice warning, "Stop doing wrong!" This time he seemed to see his own corpse. The third time the lightning came the voice commanded, "Leave your wives!" and Isaiah obeyed. Lightning struck a fourth time and Isaiah was so frightened he became ill. The same voice demanded that he leave home. Isaiah obeyed the voice and left his home. He went up and down the land to preach his religion. Crowds followed him asking to be healed and purified. A town and a mountain in Africa became sacred to his religion, and when he died the monument over his grave became sacred, too.

Isaiah Shembe's religion was based partly on the Old Testament and partly on his own experiences. His son became leader of the religion after Shembe's death.

Hundreds of other new religions are found in Africa. Africans who no longer live in tribes need a new religion to belong to, to take the place of the tribe. Africans who no longer believe in the tribal gods need a new god to believe in. Along comes someone who seems to have been miraculously cured of a disease and can cure others. A new religion is started. Or along comes someone who believes a pagan spirit or an angel has called him to preach. A new religion is started. Sometimes the new religion is similar to the old tribal religion. Sometimes it is a new Christian denomination. Sometimes it is a combination.

There are many new religions in Japan. They started when people in need could not find help in their old religion. Most of the new religions give people a group to belong to. There are new religions that have something of Shinto[1] and something of Buddhism in them. Others have something of Buddhism and something of Christianity in them. There are religions which claim to be a combination of all religions. Their leaders say, "We take the best ideas from all faiths." Most of these new religions are headed by a leader who is also a teacher. Some leaders are thought to be God, or a god, or a buddha come to earth.

There are new religions in Korea. The *Chun Do Kyo,* the "Society of Heaven," mixes ideas from Christianity and from Confucianism. It says the relationship of people to each other is most important in life. Men can reform themselves and society. Chun Do Kyo is a nationalist religion, a religion for Koreans only.

There are new religions in Southeast Asia. One of them is the *Cao Dai* in Viet Nam. Cao Dai means "Supreme Being." Cao Dai joins tribal ideas with ideas from Taoism, Buddhism, Confucianism, and Christianity. It has its own priests and its own pope. It has its own schools, and it once had its own army.

There are new religions in islands of the South Pacific. They are called *Cargo Cults.* A Cargo Cult often starts when a "prophet" comes along and announces that the world is soon coming to an end. Then God or the ancestors, he says, will bring all the things they want or need. The people build storehouses to hold this "cargo." Often they throw away their money and kill off their livestock, thinking these things will not be needed when the great day arrives with its abundant supply of new "cargo."

In the Philippine Islands the *Iglesia ni Cristo,* "Church of Christ," is a new religion with many large churches. The founder of this religion said he was an angel, a messenger of God, come to lead the church.

[1] See Chapter 1.

A new religion of south west Asia has spread to many parts of the world, especially to western nations. It is called *Baha'i*. Bab-ed-Din, a Persian Muslim, foretold that a manifestation of God would come to the people of the world. After the Bab's death his disciple, Baha-Ullah (1817-1892), said he was that manifestation of God foretold by the Bab. Baha'is believe that the coming of Baha-Ullah fulfilled the promises of the prophets of all religions. Baha'i, today, emphasizes the unity of all religions, world peace, and universal brotherhood.

There are new religions in the Americas. Many of them have their roots in Christianity. In the early part of the nineteenth century in New York State, a man named *Joseph Smith* had a series of visions in which, he said, the hiding place of a book written by a prophet called *Mormon* was revealed to him. This he translated into English, and the *Book of Mormon* became the Bible of the *Church of the Latter Day Saints* which he organized. The centre of the Mormon faith is in Salt Lake City, Utah, but its missionaries are active all over the world. Many young people pay their own expenses and give two years of their lives as missionaries in many parts of the world.

In the last quarter of the nineteenth century, a new church called the *Church of Christ, Scientist,* popularly known as "Christian Science," came into being in Boston, Massachusetts. Its founder, *Mrs. Mary Baker Eddy,* had immediately recovered her health when reading about Jesus' healings. She felt she had discovered the true meaning of the scriptures which Christians had been missing—that everything contrary to God's goodness is unreal. Therefore evil, disease, and death are unreal. They are errors of the human mind. The Bible and Mary Baker Eddy's book, *Science and Health, with Key to the Scriptures,* are the authorities for Christian Science.

Jehovah's Witnesses is a fast growing religion around the world. Jehovah's Witnesses believe Christ returned invisibly in 1914, that 144,000 people will receive life in heaven close to Christ, that a crowd of Christlike persons will receive life on earth, and that all others are doomed. "Witnesses" promise unconditional dedication to do the will of Almighty God and to obey the commandments of God, whom they call *Jehovah,* and Christ. Their meeting places, called *Kingdom Halls,* are training schools for learning how to visit and to witness. Jehovah's Witnesses do not take part in any government activity.

A group of North Americans believe that a man whom they call *Father Divine* was God living among them. He was popular in New York and Philadelphia from the nineteen twenties until the nineteen fifties. His followers gathered together on large estates, known as "heavens," where they had free meals, sang hymns of praise to Father Divine, and listened to his words of advice. They decorated the halls of the "heavens" with signs that read, "Father Divine is God," "Father Divine is King of Kings and Lord of Lords," "Father Divine is the Messiah." His followers greet each other with the word, "Peace!"

The Black Muslims are a new religion which has borrowed many religious expressions from Islam. Most of its followers are Americans of African ancestry. Black Muslims say that God, Allah, is black, that original man was black, and that black people are morally superior to other races. They claim that they are Allah's chosen people.

Other new religions in North and South America and in Europe and Asia offer health and prosperity to those who join them. A number of these religions claim to be the last religion, bringing together all the great religious teachings of the world. Many of the new religions give their followers noble ideas to guide their lives. A few demand that their followers live under strict discipline.

Substitute Religion

Some people have substitutes for religion.

One of the substitutes for religion is very old. In ancient Babylonia, where the Tigris and the Euphrates rivers flowed from the Armenian Mountains to the Persian Gulf, wise men watched the stars at night.

183

They saw that the stars moved across the sky. At different times of the night, and in different seasons of the year, the stars were in different positions. They noticed that some stars were grouped together and the stars in a group always stayed together. The movements of the stars and the star groups, they decided, must influence the lives of people.

There are people who still believe that stars have an influence on what they are, what they do, how they live. They call their belief in the stars *astrology*. Some people substitute astrology for faith in God.

There are others who make science a substitute for religion. The religion of ancient tribes was a primitive science. It attempted to meet people's needs and answer their questions about the world. Science today makes it possible to meet many human needs and to answer many questions about the universe. Therefore, some people conclude, science will, in time, meet all needs and answer all questions. Science, they say, makes religion unnecessary. So they put their hope in science and substitute faith in science for faith in God.

There are people who make their faith in humanity a substitute for religion. They say man should believe in man. In the nineteenth century in France, *Auguste Comte* said man was improving all the time and no longer needed to believe in God. Man, he said, needs only to develop himself. He needs only to believe in man. Comte started a religion of man and called it the *religion of humanity*. His followers started churches in which to sing praises to man and hear lectures on man. They believed that not only are men becoming better, wiser and stronger, but more closely united.

There are people today who say, "Man is good. He will become better. Man is the most important thing for man to live for. He needs no help from a supreme being!" These people may meet together in societies to discuss ways of helping themselves and all humanity to become better. They call themselves *humanists*. There are humanists in most parts of the world, but especially in Europe and Latin America. They often substitute faith in man for faith in God.

There are people who make loyalty to their nation a substitute for religion. *Adolf Hitler* lived in Germany in the first part of the twentieth century. When Germany was defeated in World War I, there was little food to eat and little work to be had. Adolf Hitler said to the German people, "We are suffering because of what our enemies have done to us. Let us love our country and hate our enemies. Let us show our enemies that we are stronger than they. We are the greatest people on earth." He organized big meetings and gave people slogans to shout, songs to sing, and work to do. This was German *nationalism*.

Nationalism is rather like ancient tribal religion. Tribal religions made men feel protected because everyone in the tribe worshipped the same tribal gods, who guarded them. Together they carried out tribal ceremonies to get the help of the spirit world. Nationalism makes people feel safe when everyone in the nation thinks and acts alike; and their nation becomes like a god to them. At large gatherings nationalists attempt to persuade people to make their nation strong. Nationalists consider anyone who does not believe as they do dangerous to the nation's safety. They think of God as a great being who is for them and against their enemies. Nationalism teaches people to hate the enemy. In ancient times people thought the trouble that came to the tribe was caused by evil or enemy spirits. In modern times nationalists think that a nation's troubles are due to hostile or enemy people and their sympathizers. Having an enemy who can be blamed for all the nation's troubles is an important part of nationalism. Nationalists often substitute faith in their nation for faith in God.

There are people who make pride in their race a substitute for religion. Some are believers in "white supremacy." "White supremacists" maintain that God has made white men superior to other races. Some are believers in "black nationalism." "Black nationalists" maintain that the Negro race is the purest race on earth, most like God the Creator. Belief in racial superiority is called *racism*.

Not only in the Americas, but in Africa there are some people, both "black" and "white," for whom belief in their race is rather like a modern tribal religion. There are also people in Asia who believe that their race is superior to all others.

Racists respect only people whose appearance and skin colour are similar to theirs. They look down on those whose appearance and skin colour are different from theirs. The God they believe in is a god who is like their race and favours their race. Racists often substitute belief in their own race for faith in God.

There are people who make political beliefs a substitute for religion. In the middle of the last century, in London, *Karl Marx* wrote about history, the world, and economics. His explanations about poverty and wealth seemed so clear that many people around the world thought, "Now we understand why we are poor. The rich are taking advantage of us. Karl Marx says we can fight back." Marx said history is a long story of conflicts between those who control property and those who are controlled. Those who are controlled have always been mistreated. "But," said Marx, "history is on the side of those who are mistreated. Someday they will get rid of those who misuse them, and then they will live together in a happy world."

What Marx wrote about he called *communism*. For many people communism became a substitute religion. Marx and his friend *Friedrich Engels* published *The Communist Manifesto* in 1848 which became the gospel for communists. Marx became their prophet. History—as Karl Marx explained it—became their god. The Communist Party took the place of the church. The leaders of the party were to the people like priests who told them what to do. *Lenin* was the most famous of these leaders. He led the Russian workers in a revolution in 1917 and turned Russia into a communist state. His tomb is revered as a shrine.

The Communist Party holds rallies that are substitutes for religious revivals with communist songs in place of hymns. It tries to make people feel that in communism they belong to each other—everyone is called "comrade." In group meetings people confess their "sins" against

▲   Young Buddhists listen and look for pathways to Nirvana.

▼   Young Christians worship and look for God's meaning and purpose in their lives.

the Communist Party. Communism holds classes in which the writings of Karl Marx, Lenin, and other communists are studied. Millions of people around the world have substituted faith in Marxist Communism for faith in God.

For other millions of people around the world, however, there can be no substitute for God. It was God, they say, who made the stars and fixed their place in space. So the stars themselves cannot influence lives. Scientific knowledge, they say, can make a better world but it can also destroy the world. So it is necessary for men to believe in a God who can guide them to use this knowledge in wise ways.

There are those who point out that in all those systems based on humanism without faith in God, human life is degraded and the individual person counts for nothing. Without faith in God people have nothing to unite them in goodwill. Nationalism, racism, communism divide the world. A divided world can never be a safe and happy world. Every person in the world is as important to God as every other person. God wants all people to love all others as he loves them. Only then will the world be a safe and peaceful place.

Summing
It Up

(A Comparison Chart)

The world's great religions have lasted. They have lasted because, although times may change, these religions continue to help people understand the meaning of life. They continue to meet human needs and longings. The world's religions are all alike in this. They differ, however, in their explanations. Chinese religions are concerned with a happier, longer life and getting along with each other. Important in Hinduism and Buddhism is man's search for truth. Important in Judaism, Christianity, and Islam is God's revelation to man and man's response to God. For Chinese religion, for Hinduism and Buddhism, God is outside time and history. For Judaism, Christianity, and Islam, God is active in history. For the Hindu and Buddhist, religion is a personal matter although it affects the world he lives in. For the Jew, Christian, and Muslim, religion is a social matter although it depends on the individual's response to God. Each religion is a treasure store of great ideas and inspiring thoughts.

Many thoughts and ideas in these religions are similar. Many are different, because the centre of each religion is different. The centre of a religion is what makes a difference in the way people think about their religion. The centre may be Brahman for a Hindu, the Buddha for a Buddhist, the righteous God for a Jew, Jesus Christ for a Christian, Allah for a Muslim. Only when people believe firmly in its centre can their religion have an influence on their lives and on society. When people doubt their religion, they lose the standards of character and conduct which their religion gives them.

A person who truly believes his own religion cannot believe another's

189

religion unless he twists its ideas to fit his own beliefs. However, he can believe there are good things in other religions and appreciate them. The more he learns about other religions and what they mean to the people who follow them, the better he can understand his own religion and discover what it can mean to him.

There are many varieties of beliefs in each religion. Especially is this true in Buddhism and in Hinduism. The chart on these pages shows some of the major characteristics and beliefs held by a large number of the followers of Hinduism, Southern Buddhism, Northern Buddhism, Chinese religion, Judaism, Christianity, and Islam.

GOD

Hinduism
God, unknowable, present in everyone and everything. Sometimes seen in saviour gods.

Northern Buddhism
Many saviours.

Southern Buddhism
No supreme being.

Chinese Religions
Beneficent Heaven

Judaism
One God, just and upright, demanding uprightness.

Christianity
One God, just and loving, giving love which causes people to love in turn.

Islam
One God, absolute and merciful.

MAN

Hinduism
Man, the same as, or a part of, God. Differences are not real.

Southern Buddhism
Man, a bundle of body, feelings, ideas, consciousness, thought.

Northern Buddhism
The same as Southern Buddhism.

Chinese Religions
Man, a part of the natural order of the universe.

Judaism
Man, the creation of God for his purpose.

Christianity
The same as Judaism.

Islam
Man, the creation of God to do with as he pleases in his mercy.

190

SIN

Hinduism
Sin, belief that there are differences, and attachment to them.

Southern Buddhism
Sin, clinging to life and to things.

Northern Buddhism
Same as Southern Buddhism, but not popularly emphasized.

Chinese Religions
Sin, going to extremes, losing control of oneself.

Judaism
Sin, breaking the Law of God, unfaithfulness to God.

Christianity
Sin, any act or way of life that separates man from an awareness of God.

Islam
Sin, failure to submit to God's law, faithlessness to God.

SALVATION

Hinduism
Salvation, deliverance from existence by indifference to the world, by recognition of oneness with God, or by fulfilling religious duties, or by devotion to some form of God.

Southern Buddhism
Salvation, the loss of consciousness of self forever by meditation and acts of compassion.

Northern Buddhism
Salvation, heaven where, with a saviour, one can grow towards a loss of consciousness of self. This may come through devotion to the saviour.

Chinese Religions
Salvation, living a balanced life in harmony with nature and society.

Judaism
Salvation, God's care and acceptance.

Christianity
Salvation, reconciliation with God eternally (and with all those who are reconciled).

Islam
Salvation, heaven as a reward for the faithful.

Glossary-Index[1]

Pronunciations and definitions are given if words are not found in *Webster's Seventh New Collegiate Dictionary* or if the words are used in RELIGIONS AROUND THE WORLD in a special way which may not be clear in that dictionary.

Simplified pronunciations are indicated by the following symbols: *ay* as in say; *ah* as in father; *e* or *eh* as in bet; *ee* as in me; *i* or *ih* as in sit; *igh* as in high; *o* as in on; *oh* as in go; *oo* as in moon; *ow* as in cow; *u* as in pull; *uh* as in hut. Capital letters are used to show accented syllables.

1. Pronunciations are simplified approximations to the original sound or to popular English usage. Spelling of foreign words is based on accepted patterns of transliteration except where popular English usage has already established another spelling. No stressed syllable is used for words from languages which have no stress except where English usage has established such stress.

RELIGIONS AROUND THE WORLD